# PRIOR ROGER OUTLAW OF KILMAINHAM

# Maynooth Studies in Irish Local History

SERIES EDITOR  Raymond Gillespie

This is one of six new pamphlets in the Maynooth Studies in Irish Local History Series to be published in the year 2000. Like their predecessors, most of the pamphlets are based on theses completed as part of the M.A. in local history programme in National University of Ireland, Maynooth. While the regions and time span which they cover are diverse, from Waterford to Monaghan, and from the fourteenth to the twentieth centuries, they all share a conviction that the exploration of the local past can shed light on the evolution of modern societies. They each demonstrate that understanding the evolution of local societies is important. The local worlds of Ireland in the past are as complex and sophisticated as the national framework in which they are set. The communities which peopled those local worlds, whether they be the inhabitants of religious houses, industrial villages or rural parishes, shaped and were shaped by their environments to create a series of interlocking worlds of considerable complexity. Those past worlds are best interpreted not through local administrative divisions, such as the county, but in human units: local places where communities of people lived and died. Untangling what held these communities together, and what drove them apart, gives us new insights into the world we have lost.

These pamphlets each make a significant contribution to understanding Irish society in the past. Together with twenty-eight earlier works in this series they explore something of the hopes and fears of those who lived in Irish local communities in the past. In doing so they provide examples of the practice of local history at its best and show the vibrant discipline which the study of local history in Ireland has become in recent years.

*Maynooth Studies in Irish Local History: Number 30*

# Prior Roger Outlaw
# of Kilmainham

## Eithne Massey

IRISH ACADEMIC PRESS
DUBLIN • PORTLAND, OR

First published in 2000 by
IRISH ACADEMIC PRESS
44, Northumberland Road, Dublin 4, Ireland
*and in the United States of America by*
IRISH ACADEMIC PRESS
c/o ISBS, 5804 NE Hassalo Street, Portland, OR 97213–3644.

*website*: www.iap.ie

**British Library Cataloguing in Publication Data**
Massey, Eithne
    Prior Roger Outlaw of Kilmainham. – (Maynooth studies in Irish local history; no. 30)
    1. Outlaw, Roger  2. Hospitalers – Ireland  3. Ireland – History – 1172–1603
    I. Title
    271.7'91'094183

    ISBN 0–7165–2726–X


**Library of Congress Cataloging-in-Publication Data**
Massey, Eithne.
    Prior Roger Outlaw of Kilmainham / Eithne Massey.
        p. cm.—(Maynooth studies in local history; no. 30)
    ISBN 0–7165–2726–X (pbk.)
        1. Kilmainham (Dublin, Ireland)—History.  2. Military religious orders—
    Ireland—Dublin—History—To 1500.  3. Hospitalers—Ireland—Dublin—
    History—To 1500.  4. Kilmainham (Dublin, Ireland)—Biography.
    5. Ireland—History—1172–1603.  6. Outlaw, Roger.  I. Title.  II. Series.
    DA995.D9 K486 2000
    941.8'35–dc21                                                             00–044838

Typeset in 10 pt on 12 pt Bembo by
Carrigboy Typesetting Services, County Cork
Printed by ColourBooks Ltd., Dublin

# Contents

# Acknowledgements

I would like to thank my supervisor, Dr John Bradley and the director of the M.A. course, Dr Raymond Gillespie for their kind assistance and advice while researching the material on which this study is based. I would also like to thank the staff of the National Archives and the staff of the following libraries: Maynooth University Library, the National Library of Ireland, Trinity College Library, the Royal Irish Academy, the Bodleian Library and Dublin Corporation's Gilbert Library. I acknowledge with gratitude permission to reproduce the picture of Helion de Villeneuve from the *Statuta Hospitalis Hierusalem* compiled by Friar Hugo held in the Gilbert Library, folios 4r and 114r from the Bodleian manuscript of the *Registrum* (Ms. Rawlinson B.501) and the photographs of the Hospitaller church at Hospital, Co. Limerick and Bishop Ledrede's tomb by Jacques Le Goff and Maura Leahy respectively. Thanks are also due to Emer Jackson and Ger Candon who read drafts of the original thesis and to all my companions in the M.A. class of 1997–99. Finally, I would like to thank Jacques Le Goff for his technical help and unfailing moral support.

This pamphlet is dedicated to Eileen Massey, who first told me about the Knights at Kilmainham.

# Introduction

The Order of the Knights Hospitallers of St John of Jerusalem was introduced into Ireland at some time around 1170 as an agent of support for the Anglo-Irish colony in both military and administrative terms. From its foundation in Ireland members of the order acted as administrators, bankers, gaolers, and most particularly soldiers for the Anglo-Normans and the English crown. The order's chief house of Kilmainham, Dublin, was one of eleven in Ireland, which were mainly based in Leinster and Munster. After the suppression of the Knights Templars in 1312 the Hospitallers were officially granted the Templars' houses and lands by the crown, although in many cases the actual acquisition of these lands was achieved with difficulty. The number of Hospitaller houses increased to seventeen and the importance of the order, both as a land-holder and an agent of the crown, was accordingly augmented. The history of the order in Ireland is closely linked to the fortunes of the Anglo-Irish colony. The important role it played in the politics of the time – through its wealth, it military importance and the many priors who acted as high officials in the Dublin administration – has been somewhat underplayed in the histories of the period. This study will examine the career of one of these priors: the fourteenth-century Roger Outlaw, in the context of the community of the Kilmainham manor. It will be seen that the fortunes of the man and the manor were inextricably linked.

The Order of the Knights Hospitallers was founded in Jerusalem towards the end of the eleventh century and had as its original functions care of the sick and the provision of hospitality to pilgrims. Later, its role extended to defence of these same pilgrims. As time went on, the order became more and more militaristic and by the early fourteenth century the main aim of the Hospitaller knights was battle with the Moslem armies of Mediterranean Europe and Latin Syria. In some countries their original task of the provision of hospitality had been transformed to a large degree into the corrody or pension system, which provided long-term lodging to wealthy individuals in exchange for money or favours. After the fall of Jerusalem in 1187 the order moved its headquarters to Acre. In 1291 the fall of Acre resulted in the Hospitallers setting up their main house in Limassol, finally moving to Rhodes in 1309. In terms of the order as a whole, the function of the Irish priory was essentially to provide finance for the campaigns of the knights in the near east. At the head of the order was the grand master, who throughout most of Outlaw's time was Fra Helion de Villeneuve, and below him a huge and highly structured multi-national organisation stretching from the Middle East to its western reaches in Ireland. The order was divided into sections called '*langues*' or 'tongues' according to the language of its members, with the Irish priory coming under the English langue and officially under the control of the Grand Priory at Clerkenwell. In practice, during Outlaw's priorship, there seems to have been a great deal of independence on the part of the Irish section of the order. Within the Irish context the order's role had been modified to that of major landowner and standing army for the colony. By the time of Roger Outlaw, the Hospitallers' role as trusted officials to the king was undisputed and while the highest administrative post in Ireland – that of justiciar – was generally the preserve of nobles or special favourites of the monarch, the priors of the order had often held other important roles in the administration.

The order was divided into three classes – chaplains, knights and serjeants, and as only those of knightly blood could be confirmed at the higher levels, anyone of Gaelic blood was effectively barred from reaching any prominence in the order. At the head of the Irish section or priory was the prior and below him the various preceptors, including the preceptor of Kilmainham who was responsible for the management of the house and its accompanying lands. These were the local administrators of the Hospitaller properties, who acted as witnesses to the grants and agreements made by the order. The members of the order met at regular chapters to confirm these grants – held not just at Kilmainham but at different houses in Ireland. During Outlaw's time as prior there were ten of these. It was a highly structured, rigid community. The size and physical scope of the order had always meant that it had to be firmly bureaucratic in terms of its record-keeping: as early as 1262 each prior was required to compile a register of properties under his jurisdiction. The statutes of 1239[1] list rigid controls on dress, on habits, even on behaviour at the table. The long list of commands against disorderly speech, slandering other brothers, drawing blood from a colleague (except from the nose or mouth) and other rowdy behaviour indicates that the order functioned as a military rather than a religious entity and also testifies to the difficulties which must have arisen when a group of hardened soldiers were lodged together.

By the second decade of the fourteenth century, when Roger Outlaw became prior of the Irish Hospitallers, the order had established itself as an integral and important part of the colony. It was a colony under threat, however. Historians cite the Bruce invasion, the Gaelic advances, the on-going feuding between the Anglo-Irish magnates and, after Outlaw's death, the Black Death as factors in the 'decline' of the lordship in the fourteenth century. This emphasis on 'decline' ignores the fact that, at least in the first half of the century, the disorder and confusion of the time in a way facilitated individuals such as Outlaw in the acquisition of wealth and power. Under his priorship, the Hospitaller order, an integral part of the colony, did not decline, but rather increased in importance. In addition, in a country where the annalists speak of constant unrest and famine, the affairs of the Hospitaller manors, as mirrored through the *Registrum*, reflect an orderly world where the community – including all levels of society from grandees to stable-hands – celebrates feasts such as Christmas with banquets and lavish gifts.

It is against this background that Outlaw began his career as prior. That he managed to achieve so much in a period of on-going conflict, war and famine, while owing loyalty to a wide range of masters, is a reflection of the shrewdness of his methods. The corrody system, based on long term maintenance in return for money or services, played an important role in this process and this will be demonstrated when we examine closely the community at Kilmainham. By exploring how the community functioned as a social entity it will become clear how the daily life of those who lived there was governed by a strict system of internal rights, privileges and obligations. These rigidly set laws and hierarchical structures must have acted as both a source of restriction and a source of security to its inmates. But first it will be useful to look at the physical space which religious and laity shared at Kilmainham.

# The community at Kilmainham:
# the world of the manor

The main sources of information on the community and buildings of Kilmainham are the fourteenth century *Registrum de Kilmainham*[1] and the *Extents of Irish Monastic Possessions*[2] dating from the 1540s. The *Extents* provide a clear picture of Kilmainham at the time of the dissolution of the religious houses in Ireland, but it would be dangerous to assume that there had been no changes in the physical structure and layout of the house since the time of the *Registrum*. The *Registrum* exists as a single copy in its original form and is held in the Bodleian library at Oxford where it is classed B.501 of the Rawlinson collection. A Latin transcription is available in print and there is a manuscript English translation held in the Royal Irish Academy.[3] The material included in it covers all the Hospitallers' houses in Ireland but a significant percentage is concerned with their main house at Kilmainham. The *Registrum* is essentially an official record of the contracts made between the Hospitallers and various individuals during the period 1321–50. Each transaction is recorded as a separate entry and notes the name of the person involved and the details of the agreement. The vast bulk of the entries deal with corrodies and land rentals, although there are also some entries dealing with benefices to members of the order.

The *Registrum* provides a wealth of information on Kilmainham. From it it is clear that the official residence of the Irish prior consisted of a great hall,[4] one or more churches,[5] dormitories,[6] several rooms or *camerae* where guests were lodged[7] and an assortment of other buildings. These buildings included dwelling-houses which could be the homes of either guests or servants and which in many cases were built by the lodgers themselves.[8] There was an inner walled enclosure with fortified towers on each corner and a gatehouse under the eastern tower: within this space were the main buildings of the Kilmainham complex.[9] Beyond this and enclosing the manor of Kilmainham were outer walls with a main gate facing south towards what was then the common green of Kilmainham.[10] There are few references to Kilmainham village as a separate entity from the manor, although an entry in the justiciary rolls of 1312 indicates that there was a gallows nearby.[11] The village itself was Hospitaller property as both the *Extents* and references to 'our vill of Kilmainham' in the *Registrum* show.[12] Some of the servants lived in the village of Kilmainham and in the case of sickness, could arrange to have their meals brought to them there.[13] The manor would thus have constituted the social and economic focus of the surrounding district. The Hospitaller lands extended over a large area, west from what is now Bow Bridge as far east as Chapelizod, including the area between the Liffey and the Camac rivers, and stretching northwards beyond the Liffey to encompass much of what is now the Phoenix Park.[14] While there are no walls of the manor left standing, it seems likely that the inner enclosure of the Great Hall stood on the high ground at Inchicore Road between the two river valleys – perhaps around the area of what is now the western entrance to the Royal Hospital. This was a perfect defensive site. It had a good outlook and was protected by rivers, with access to water for domestic use, milling and fishing.[15] Both weirs on the Liffey and mills on the much smaller Camac appear to have been important to the economy of the manor. The site was well wooded, and therefore supplied with fuel and building materials. It stood in the path of major routes from the south and west, just beyond the walls of Dublin. No evidence of the buildings of this period remain but the more important ones were certainly built of stone.[16] It has been speculated that the sandstone blocks exposed during the renovation of the Royal Hospital originally came from the priory.[17]

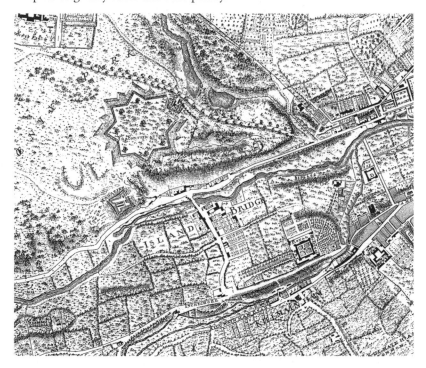

*1.* Kilmainham. Rocque Map of 1756.
(Source: National Library of Ireland, *Historic Dublin Maps* (Dublin 1988))

These references to the various buildings and physical features at Kilmainham help to construct a picture of the living conditions of the manor at the time. There were a large number of working buildings – dairies,[18] dormitories,[19] stables,[20] breweries, and forges.[21] There was a drawbridge under the great eastern tower[22] and the great sewer and a cesspool are also mentioned.[23] There was a prison,[24] the *tetra domus de malrepos* – the dismal house of little ease – built near the walls, and there were also fishponds,[25] shrubberies,[26] and orchards[27] while the walls themselves appear to been wide enough to provide an area of recreation.[28] There is also a reference to the *domus stauri*[29] which appears to have been a stock house. There are constant references to permission being given for both servants and guests to extend their accommodation or in some cases build new houses[30] and the Hospitallers themselves engaged in construction, erecting new buildings, including a new burning-house *(novum oustrenam)*,[31] and dormitory.[32] Some of this building may have been a necessary result of the Bruce wars and the attendant disorder, but unlike other priories in the city Kilmainham does not seem to have been attacked. It seems more likely that the on-going building was a sign of economic development and recovery.

In the *Extents* there is a reference to the church at Kilmainham which was a parochial as well as a conventual church and which the compiler notes is now too large to be kept up by the impoverished population of the village.[33] Churches are mentioned in the *Registrum* as part of the manor but no indication is given as to where they stood. If the knights followed the usual medieval practice it is likely that the church and the burial ground stood to the west of the living quarters, but the rather indistinct cross in Girdler's (admittedly much later) map of 1655 (figure 2) seems to indicate that this was not the case. It is possible that the cross marks a subsidiary chapel attached to the manor rather than the remains of the original main church. Tiles dating from the period were dug up in Bully's Acre in 1859 and exhibited at the Royal Irish Academy.[34] Reading the *Registrum*, one senses that the church was not the main focus of attention in the lives of the Hospitallers. Rather, the great hall where the brothers met and ate under the eye of the prior was the centre of community life in the order. To understand why this was the case it is necessary to examine in some depth how the community at Kilmainham functioned as a social entity.

Society at Kilmainham was based on the corrody system, whereby in exchange for money or services individuals were given long-term maintenance at the manor. The corrody system was common in many religious houses in this period, although rarely to the extent it operated at Kilmainham. It can be seen as an early form of life assurance; corrodians were guaranteed the security of maintenance even when they were old and infirm. Barbara Harvey's study of the monks of Westminster Abbey contains a section on corrodies, but the system there did not operate in the same way, nor was it in any sense so important to the community. She does make the interesting point that if cash rather than land was the method of payment for the corrodies the system must often have resulted in the monks living beyond their means.

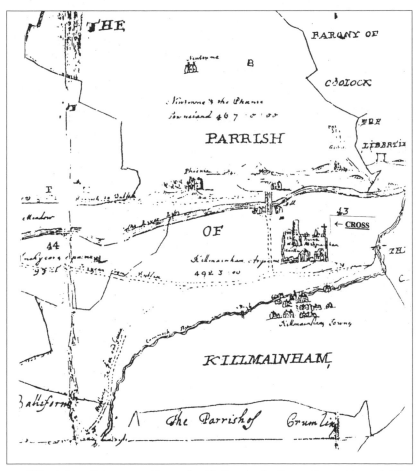

2. Kilmainham Priory 1654. Drawn by Girdler for the Down Survey. Source NLI.

The corrody system was an extremely hierarchical one, with treatment based on the level of service or financial recompense offered. The corrody entries usually consist of a commitment to provide board and lodging and a robe and hose, all of a certain level depending on the individual's contribution to the order. This ranged from bare subsistence for an individual who was provided with the cheapest robe and a place at the table of the free servants to the grandeur of such lodgers as Walter de Islep and his retinue of servants.

Four classes of corrody can be distinguished: at grade A or 'Grandee' status, the lodger was seated at the prior's table, presented annually with a robe which could be valued at over 40 shillings, given lodging for servants and horses and usually allowed many other special privileges. Grade B or 'VIP' corrodies were provided for those who were seated at the table of the esquires and brothers, allowed to keep servants and provided with clothing of the standard of the brothers of the order. The conditions of those at Grade C or 'Brother/Esquire' level were similar, except that they did not keep servants. As well as paying guests and those who provided such professional services as legal advocacy, one or two of the higher servants, such as the cook at Kilmainham, were granted corrodies at this level.[35] Finally, there was the lowest level, Grade D or 'Servant' level. In most cases these were provided to individuals acting in some way in the service of the brothers at the level of janitor[36] or smith[37] for example. The rare charity case is also included at this level.

The distribution of the entries on corrodies in the *Registrum* (Table 1) gives us a clear picture of the importance of Kilmainham in its role as the order's main centre of lodging and maintenance.

*Table 1*    Distribution of Corrodies throughout Hospitaller Order

| | Grade A | Grade B | Grade C | Grade D | Total |
|---|---|---|---|---|---|
| Kilmainham | 9 | 16 | 5 | 19 | 49 |
| Any | 0 | 2 | 4 | 7 | 13 |
| Kilmainhambeg | 0 | 1 | 2 | 5 | 8 |
| Tully | 0 | 2 | 1 | 5 | 8 |
| Killergy | 0 | 1 | 1 | 5 | 7 |
| Ard | 0 | 1 | 1 | 1 | 3 |
| Baliscoak | 0 | 2 | 2 | 0 | 4 |
| Clontarf | 0 | 0 | 2 | 5 | 7 |
| Clonaul | 0 | 0 | 0 | 1 | 1 |
| Killele | 0 | 0 | 0 | 1 | 1 |
| Kilbarry | 0 | 0 | 0 | 1 | 1 |
| Total | 09 | 25 | 18 | 50 | 102 |

*Source: Registrum de Kilmainham*

This table shows only those entries where it has been possible to assign a financial value to the corrody and grade it A, B, C or D. If the relative value of the corrodies is calculated, it appears that not only did Kilmainham have the highest number of corrodies, but it was also the one with corrodies of the highest value. While it had 49 per cent of the overall number of corrodies when this is expressed in monetary terms this corresponds to 68 per cent of the value of corrodies made. The Kilmainham house was clearly highly dependant on the corrody system as a source of income and social status. Interestingly, the *Registrum* does not show a comparable situation in relation to the entries on lands leased – there are very few entries concerning Kilmainham and the value of lands leased is low. As, according to the *Extents*, the lands at Kilmainham were extensive and fertile, it seems likely that much of them were farmed by the brothers and their servants in order to supply the Hospitallers and their guests with food. The *Registrum* presents a picture of a community at Kilmainham which was based on the important clients who stayed at the manor rather than on farming the lands. The main business of the manor and its employees centres around the presence of these great magnates, their needs and activities, their comings and goings and rights and privileges. Similarly, the lack of references to leases on mills, which was common practice in relation to other houses, indicates that the Hospitallers at Kilmainham acted as millers themselves, perhaps providing the manor with its food supply.

Looking at the figures for Kilmainham itself it can be seen that the number of corrodians at VIP level is not far below (sixteen as compared to nineteen) the grants given to servants. However, one should perhaps be wary of basing too many assumptions about the number of servants employed at the manors on the data in the *Registrum*. It appears that the relatively low number of grants to servants is the result of a situation whereby it was only servants of a certain status who were given the security of having their position recorded in writing. The corrodies at higher level contain numerous references to the servants kept by the corrodians, and included horse-boys and domestic servants, so the servant population at Kilmainham must have been quite high, constituting a whole sub-culture within the manor. Unfortunately the limitations in the sources prevent identification of most of these individual servants or even information on whether they came from the local community. The distribution of entries on various trades and crafts at Kilmainham show references only to the more skilled workmen, or at least to those with a high level of responsibility.[38] There were a wide variety of functions attached to the house – grangekeepers,[39] keepers of the water,[40] carpenters,[41] farriers[42] and butlers[43] are all listed. As already mentioned, the cook of Kilmainham is given esquire status in his corrody. The provision of food and beer to the higher-level corrodians appears to have been lavish. The single interesting limitation on provisions was that unlike the English priory at this time, no wine was drunk at Kilmainham. Here again the importance of the hospitality function to the Kilmainham house can be seen. If the house was to be known as a centre of luxury, provisions had to be generous and the master-chef needed to be treated with respect.

In terms of the Hospitaller order's assigned role as carers of the sick, there is an interesting lack of references to physicians in the Kilmainham entries, unlike the house at Any, where Maurice Kermerdyn is described as a *fiscius*.[44] There is a reference to a grant to John Son of Ralph, chaplain of the house of the sick of the Blessed Laurence near Dublin, which most authorities have taken to be the leper-house of St Laurence at Chapelizod.[45] There is also a reference to a barber who McNeill suggests could be a barber-surgeon because of his generous corrody.[46] Maria Fitzsimons speculates that the reference to the prison may indicate that the Hospitallers took care of the insane as well as holding prisoners,[47] although given the military nature of the house it seems more likely that hostages rather than the mentally ill were kept there. Nonetheless, care of the sick was from the early days of the order considered an important part of the duties of the Hospitallers. The Rule of the Hospital stated the responsibilities of the order towards the sick, including the provision of good food and comfortable bedding.[48] The Norman French version of the Rule which dates from the first quarter of the fourteenth century and was in the keeping of the Hospitaller preceptory at Kilbarry in Waterford goes even further, stating: 'the sick and the needy are the lords and we, who are the Hospitallers, are their servants.'[49] The complete lack of evidence of this kind of activity in Kilmainham may be an indication of how far removed from the ideals of the order the Hospitallers in Kilmainham had come. *Reportorium Viride*, the early sixteenth century list of churches for the Dublin diocese compiled by Archbishop John Alen, describes Kilmainham as '*zenodochium, non autem elemosaria infirmorum*' (i.e. a guesthouse, not a charitable hospital) – '*(ut supra in altero hospitali Sancti Johannis Baptiste) sed peregrinorum et hospitum.*'[50] It seems that St John the Baptist's, a charitable house of the Crutched Friars outside the walls of Dublin at Newgate had acquired the task of care of the infirm.

Among the names of those who were connected to the house at Kilmainham none appear to be of Gaelic origin. This is reflected in the manors of the knights throughout Ireland – out of 297 entries only six are Gaelic names.[51] Many of the names are associated with a craft and there is an interesting reference to the farrier, David de Slebeche: Slebeche was one of the order's houses in Pembrokeshire.[52] There is little other indication of servants moving between the different houses of the order although an exception is the case of Robert son of Thomas the Reve, who in 1333 is recorded as having been given the position of farm bailiff in St John's in Ards and in 1338 was granted a corrody of a higher value in his role as keeper of the grange and the river at Kilmainham.[53] If, as seems highly likely, these records refer to the same person, it can be seen that physical and social mobility were at least possibilities in the lives of the free servants.

Women do not figure highly in the *Registrum*: there are only fourteen entries which refer to them and in the main these concern the wives of those who are servants or corrodians of the house, as in the case of Cecilia, wife of Hugh de Nassynton.[54] The corrody concerning Alice La Reve and her daughter Mathilda is unusual, referring as it does both to a woman and to a charity case. In return for their piety in assisting with divine praises, the pair are promised maintenance from the house of Kilmainham for life, to be provided in the form of bread, beer and a daily dish from the kitchen:

> *Nouerit uniuersitas uestra nos unamimi assensu et uoluntate nostra caritatis intuitu et diuini amoris contemplacione concessisse Alicie dicte la Reue et Matilde filie sue que diuinis preconiis intendere assistunt pro sustentacione sua quoaduixerint cotidianam liberacionem de domo nostra de Kilmaynan, uideliciet unius panis albi et alterius bisi duarum lagenarum melioris ceruisie et unius ferculi de coquina.*[55]

Charity cases in general do not figure largely in the *Registrum*: perhaps because they were not of a contractual basis. This may also be the reason why there are no references to pilgrims staying at the order's houses: again the contract would have been a short-term one, not of enough significance to be included in the *Registrum*. Pilgrims of a certain class did visit Kilmainham, as is recorded later in the fourteenth century.[56] There is an occasional reassurance of care for the aged or infirm. Brother John de Kirketon for example, was so concerned about his future security that an undertaking was made that he should be lodged in the house at Kilmainham until the end of his days, '*Nec absque mero ipsius arbitrio ad locum alium artetur amouendus.*'[57]

At the other end of the scale from Alice La Reve and John de Kirketon, there were the grandees of Kilmainham, those privileged guests who were lodged in a style which can only be described as magnificent. Even the language used in the *Registrum* reflects the importance of these men: it is much more elaborate and the entries are far longer. Nine individuals were granted corrodies at this level at Kilmainham, although in many cases there is more than one entry dealing with the same corrodian as his treatment was improved as time went on. While the Hospitallers' statutes of 1239 portray a way of life which was austere and inflexible, with severe restrictions on speech and action,[58] and the draconian *karantine* (a forty-day fast) imposed for serious transgressions, it appears that those holding the grander corrodies in the Kilmainham house were not subject to such constraints. William le Mareschal was one such corrodian. His position in the Kilmainham house was upgraded on a regular basis throughout the period covered in the *Registrum*. While this was presumably mainly because of favours, monetary payments and possibly gifts of land, it was also not unconnected with his brother John's rise to power and influence – John was preceptor at Kilmainhambeg in Meath during much of the period covered in the *Registrum* and after the death of Roger Outlaw he was elected prior for a short time.[59] Equally, John's rise was no doubt connected with his brother's generosity to the order. William le Mareschal's corrody included a place at the prior's table, a robe with four trimmings and furs, provision for numerous servants and horses and as time went on exceptional privileges. These included permission to eat in his room whenever he wished (generally individuals staying at the house were only excused from attendance at the great hall by reason of age or infirmity), to eat meat when the brothers were fasting, to have his own chaplain serve him in his private chapel and to freely move himself and his goods in and out of the manor.[60] The privilege of moving freely in and out of Kilmainham was obviously highly prized, while the number of references to individual lodgers being allowed to move their possessions in and out of the house makes one wonder if the good brothers were inclined to retain worldly goods once these were taken into their charge.[61] The personal possessiveness forbidden to members of the order was possibly re-directed towards the acquisition of communal goods in the same way that the pursuit of personal power and influence could be sublimated to the pursuit of the order's interests. The acquisition of goods or land for the order was the normal way in which members of the Hospitallers in Ireland advanced their careers. References like these, together with the ongoing presence of such wealthy, worldly lodgers as Walter de Islep, give us a picture of a community where the religious ethos was highly coloured by close contact with the secular world. The corrody itself could be treated as a commodity: Hugh de Saltu, granted his corrody for legal services and advocacy, sold it to William de Cicestre.[62]

So what was the attraction for those who decided to lodge at Kilmainham? There were undoubtedly a number of reasons why guests availed of the corrody system. There was the security of high walls and a resident army in the wake of the Bruce wars and its accompanying unrest and famine (Ireland suffered repeated and serious crop failures and shortages during the period 1294–1348);[63] the comfort of knowing that one would be looked after in old age, the very human delight in the connection with a powerful elite and the opportunities and entertainment afforded by being at the centre of political scheming and gossip. The house may also have functioned as a refuge and sanctuary for those no longer in favour such as the disgraced treasurer Walter de Islep. Its location, close to the hub of Dublin yet far enough away from the city to be a pleasant riverside environment added to its attractions. Any guilt that a guest might have felt at the luxury of the treatment meted out to him would have been counter-balanced by the knowledge that he was living in a house of God and his spiritual as well as material welfare was being looked after. The *Registrum* contains frequent references to masses being said not only for the corrody holders themselves, but also for their families and ancestors.[64] This pre-occupation with religion did not preclude belief in charms, incantations and phylacteries, which dealt with such practical matters as how to keep rats and mice out of standing corn. Charms such as these are found in contemporary manuscripts which were held at the Hospitaller house in Kilbarry.[65] The Hospitallers' Rule or *Riwle*, also held at Kilbarry, also gives a long account of the various apocryphal miracles associated with the main 'Holy House of the Hospital' at Jerusalem, so that insofar as the order can be said to have a particular symbolic focus, that focus was on the institution of the *house* rather than on a patron saint[66] or the founder of the order. The concept of the 'House' as the safe, enclosed space where the members came together under the leadership of the prior seems to have been at the centre of the Hospitallers' feelings of identification with the community.

While the provision of sumptuous meals, a favoured place at table and magnificent robes with numerous furs and trimmings acted as an attraction to guests, the system also bound these guests more closely to the community at Kilmainham. Historians of private life in the Middle Ages have stressed the importance of outward show – gesture, clothes, feasting – as an expression of power and a form of social control.[67] This is a clear example of this. The clothes given out by the prior at Christmas were of different levels of magnificence but were probably of a uniform cut and appearance, and bound the wearer more tightly in allegiance to the house, while declaring the status of the order in the streets of Dublin.[68] In a similar way, the gathering of all the inhabitants of Kilmainham into the great hall to eat must have acted as a unifying mechanism for laity and religious alike. One of the greatest privileges which appears in the *Registrum* is permission not to attend the hall but eat alone or with companions in one's own room. Because of the rigid nature of the structure of the community, these special favours held a great significance – if the power to enforce sanctions is one of the greatest indicators of power in a community, the power to allow privileges and exemptions from normal duties is almost equally meaningful.

It is clear that the guests themselves were happy with being identified with the Kilmainham house and that they themselves wanted this feeling of belonging, of connection with what was, after all, a rich and powerful group of men. Many of those who took up the opportunity of attaching themselves to the order may not have had a family to provide the dynastic links and security for the future which were economic and social necessities of the time. Some of them may have been men who had risen socially in the recent past, as the large number of bureaucrats and record-keepers living at Kilmainham indicates. And this worked both ways: the knights were forbidden by their vow of chastity from forging the direct dynastic bonds with other families which Robin Frame sees as part and parcel of the way the colony functioned.[69] They therefore had to have the ability to produce their own networks, with links made of friendship in arms, political favour and generous treatment. Prior

Roger Outlaw demonstrated these abilities to such an extent that the community at Kilmainham can be seen as developing along particular lines as a result of his vision. This does not mean that Outlaw was unaware of family ties – indeed the opposite was the case – but much of his energy during his career seems to have gone into creating and maintaining links with the rich and powerful who were not bound by ties of kinship. For someone in Outlaw's position, deeply involved in the politics of the Lordship, this network would have acted to some degree to counter-balance the power of the great magnate families which were on the ascendant at this time. Kilmainham, as a centre of lavish hospitality in a time when 'falsehood and famine and homicide filled the country, and undoubtedly men ate each other in Ireland'[70] played a key role in this policy. How important this role was will be demonstrated when we look more closely at the relationship between the manor of Kilmainham and other institutions and individuals in the city of Dublin, a relationship that was closely bound up with the career of Roger Outlaw.

# The world beyond the manor

Roger Outlaw's career encompassed roles as churchman, administrator, soldier and diplomat. In this way he was not unusual for his time: what is remarkable is the facility with which he appears to have been able to move from one role to another, and his ability to create strong bonds with the individuals who made up these different social networks. Outlaw's family had reached prominence in the eastern part of Ireland and particularly in Kilkenny by the early fourteenth century.[1] There may have been an on-going family connection with the Hospitallers and certainly after Outlaw's rise to prominence these connections are in evidence: Richard Outlaw is listed as preceptor of Kilmainhambeg from 1328 to 1334[2] and Arnauld Outlaw as a tenant for land at the new castle at Strathleuelyn (near Kilmainhambeg Co. Meath) from 1335.[3] Falkiner states that Roger Outlaw was prior of the Hospital from 1311,[4] but there is some doubt as to this date as Walter del Aqua is still listed as the prior of the Hospital in the justiciary rolls of 1314.[5] However, Outlaw is mentioned as a brother in the order in a legal case against Thomas de Snyterby as early 1308.[6] It is likely that he became prior of the Hospital in Ireland in or around 1315, taking over from del Aqua who still continued to be involved in the military activities of the order. Del Aqua was assigned by the justiciar in 1315 to help in the defence of the citizens of Dublin, 'in order to suppress the malice of the Scottish and Irish felons.'[7] By 1314 Outlaw himself had reached some prominence in military terms. He is one of the long list of nobles and clerics who are addressed by Edward II, encouraging them to continue being stalwart in their defence of Ireland against the Scots.[8]

Paralleling Outlaw's rise within the Kilmainham community he also became an important figure in the national administration. By 1317 he is listed as deputy for the treasurer Walter de Islep,[9] and is also pardoned for appropriating land without licence.[10] Pardons to Outlaw for acquiring land in mortmain or without a licence will appear frequently throughout his career, specifically in relation to the acquisition of the rights to churches. By 1322 Outlaw is chancellor,[11] a post he was to hold with very little interruption until his death in 1341. The chancellorship was one of the most stable of the Anglo-Irish administrative posts and it was held on a regular basis by members of the Hospitaller order throughout the fourteenth century. The role of the chancellor was that of second-in-command to the most powerful official in Ireland, the justiciar, and the position entailed long periods acting as deputy

during the justiciar's absences in England. Among the main responsibilities of
the chancellor would have been the keeping of records and the issuing of legal
writs. In 1323 Outlaw travelled to England, as a special messenger and with
Archbishop Bicknor of Dublin put forward the dangerous state of the colony
to the king.[12] Here we see Outlaw and Bicknor operating as allies for the first
time in a connection which was to be upheld throughout Outlaw's career. On
his return in 1324 he became once again deputy treasurer for Walter de Islep
for a short period.[13] The first mention of Outlaw leading a military campaign
is in 1326 when the exchequer lists his fees for men going to Ulster to take
into the king's hands the lands of the late earl of Ulster and to 'restore peace
to the lands in a state of war *(terris guerrinis)* there, to take hostages for keeping
the peace from the English and Irish of that land.'[14] A further reference in the
same year to Outlaw's expenses in going to Ulster to 'treat with the men of
Ulster and look into their hearts *(et eorum corda scutanda)'*[15] would seem to
indicate that he was valued as a diplomat as well as a soldier. Again, in 1327 he
was sent west to treat with O'Connor of Connacht.[16] In 1331 Outlaw once
more travelled to England to inform the king of the problems of the
Lordship,[17] but by 1332 he was back in Ireland. In this year he was once again
engaged in extensive travelling, this time within the Anglo-Norman colony,
as he is listed as being owed expenses for journeys to Kildare, Carlow,
Tipperary, Kilkenny, Waterford, Cork and Limerick 'to treat for the
improvement of the peace'.[18] Outlaw was obviously trusted in his capacity as
negotiator, but his position also involved somewhat more brutal duties, as the
references in the exchequer rolls to payment due to him for organising the
beheading of a certain Nicholas Lomp, king's felon[19] and the costs of holding
hostages[20] indicate. In 1334–5 he travelled to both Ulster and Connacht in
what seems to have been an extensive campaign of parleying with the Irish,
among them the O'Neills, the McCartans, O'Moores, O'Dempseys,
O'Connors, O'Tooles, the Mc Murroughs and the O'Reillys.[21]

While Outlaw's skills as soldier and negotiator appear to have been put to
continuous use there were two occasions when he was removed from the
office of chancellor. One was in May 1331, when he was commanded to give
up the chancery rolls to Adam de Lymberg. Outlaw travelled to London the
following August in what was probably an attempt to consolidate his position
as well as a mission to inform the king of the state of government in Ireland.[22]
By the autumn of 1332 Lymberg was commanded to return the rolls to
Outlaw[23] and it is possible he never actually took up office. Thomas
Charleton, bishop of Hereford, took over the post in 1337[24] but on his
promotion to justiciar in 1338 Outlaw was again appointed chancellor and
held the position until his death in February 1341.[25] This return to favour may
be not unconnected with the fact that in this year also Outlaw was helping the
finances of the king with a loan of £200.[26] In addition to his post as

chancellor, Outlaw was the deputy justiciar for John Darcy throughout much of that individual's career. He held the post during Darcy's sojourns away from Ireland for periods in 1317, 1327–30, 1335–7, and 1340–1.[27] Although Darcy was never a corrody holder at Kilmainham his connection with Outlaw was a close one: as he is listed in the *Register*, along with John Morice, Robert le Poer and Dean Rodeyard as a witness to a grant of land to John Plunkett.[28]

Outlaw's activity in the king's service did not mean he was unable to promote the interests of the order of Hospitallers in Ireland, particularly by the acquisition of land. The Hospitallers were going through a period of disorder and upheaval at this time, with Leonard de Tibertis sent by the grand master to enquire into irregularities in both Ireland and England: he was given safe-conduct and the assistance of local sheriffs to do so, the king having been informed that:

> some persons, brothers of the Hospital and others, scheming to hinder the reformation of the estate of the Hospital and to avoid due correction, have eloigned the goods of the Hospital . . . and do not intend to obey the said brother Leonard duly: the king, wishing to assist Leonard . . . in order that the estate of the Hospital, which is now miserably depressed, may be reformed, orders the sheriff to go to Leonard when requested by him.[29]

As there is nothing in the records to indicate that Leonard ever reached Ireland, it would seem that Outlaw was left in complete control of the order there. He was very actively engaged in Hospitaller business, so much so that the earl of Kildare complained to the king in 1328 that the prior could not aid or counsel him, as he was too occupied with the business of the hospital and with care of his widespread possessions.[30]

From 1319, when Archbishop Bicknor agreed to the rights of the Hospitallers to the Church at Rathmore,[31] Outlaw was active in acquiring lands and benefices for the order. The acquisition of the Templar lands, which was such a difficult task in England and elsewhere, became one of the main aims of Outlaw's career. As early as 1317 he was appealing to the pope to ensure that the Hospitallers obtain these lands, as the papal mandate of that year demonstrates.[32] Problems with acquisition of the Templar possessions continued: a letter from Pope John XXII, dated 1320, gives a litany of complaints against ecclesiastics, nobles and others who have attacked both the property and the persons of the Hospital and carried away its goods. The pope ordered restitution for these attacks. Many of these illegal acquisitions were probably goods and livestock attached to the Templar properties. On the evidence of the *Registrum*, Outlaw appears to have been ultimately successful in acquiring a great deal of Templar properties. He managed to procure an interest in the preceptories of Clontarf, Crook, Clonaul, Kilsaran, Killergy and Kilbarry, all of which were Templar foundations. Outlaw was careful to ensure that such acquisitions were recorded and witnessed, as the very existence of the *Registrum* signifies.

In some cases Outlaw appears to have seized the property without permission from the king: acquisitions without a licence or in mortmain are recorded for the years 1317,[33] 1318,[34] 1327[35] and 1338.[36] In this area he seems to have operated on the premise that it is easier to obtain absolution than permission. In addition, there are also a number of commands to Outlaw to return lands which he had been holding in trust to their rightful owners – for example the lands originally held by Hugh Despenser[37] and Hugh de Audelye,[38] indicating that the prior was sometimes possessive of property once it came within his control.

In 1338, the king rewarded Outlaw for long service and his recent loan of money with the custody of the manor of Salmon Leap, or Leixlip.[39] Outlaw died at the preceptory of Any (Knockainy, Co. Limerick) in February 1341. He was active in the political life of Ireland right up to the time of his death.

Certain themes emerge from even this brief summary of Outlaw's career: the acquisition of lands for the Hospitallers, the military prowess in the service of the king and the diplomatic skills which were demonstrated in his negotiations with both the Irish and the feuding Anglo-Norman magnates. Despite efforts to remove him from his central position in the power structure of Ireland, he held onto a position of great authority to the end of his life. He appears to have been a man who was too firmly entrenched in the local political community to be easily dislodged, and through the examination of the web of personal contacts he managed to establish (most of them corrody holders at Kilmainham) some of the reasons for this will become apparent.

The power elite of Dublin at the time was a small, tightly knit circle, suspicious of outsiders sent directly from the king's court. This suspicion was often justified, as these officials were commonly sent to check the implementation of the king's wishes and the collection of the king's taxes.[40] However, as time went on, many of these outsiders became insiders and as adept as the native administrators at using Dublin's distance from the crown to further their own interests. Outlaw, as chancellor for a large part of his career and as a regular acting justiciar, had ample opportunity to make contact with these senior officials. Indeed he managed to be on such good terms with them that many of them became corrody holders at Kilmainham. Of the twenty-eight holders of the most valuable grades of corrody at the manor, eleven are listed in the records of government. Some were lawyers and legal officials, some were clerics, some held high offices in the Dublin adminis-tration. Many held the role of both cleric and administrator, like Outlaw himself. Hugh de Nassyngton,[41] Hugh de Saltu,[42] William Le Mareschal,[43] William Bodyn,[44] William Boseworth,[45] John de Grauntsete,[46] John de

3. Stained glass window in St John's Church, Hospital, showing the original Hospitaller Church where Roger Outlaw is buried. Photograph Jacques Le Goff.

Horewode,[47] Walter de Kynefare,[48] William de Wideworth,[49] William de Bardelby[50] and Walter de Islep[51] all appear in government records and as corrody holders. Within the remit of this circle one figure must be added, although he did not hold a corrody at Kilmainham. This is the figure of Alexander Bicknor, archbishop of Dublin and one-time treasurer, who was closely connected with Outlaw both directly (notably in their mutual antipathy to the bishop of Ossory) and indirectly through his long and close association with Walter de Islep. The career of de Islep will be examined in detail, for it sheds an interesting light on the society at Kilmainham.

Walter de Islep was the recipient of the most magnificent corrody granted at Kilmainham, and therefore by the Hospitallers in Ireland. His privileges were enormous, and by 1338 included permission to move his goods freely in and out freely of the Hospital and sit, not just at the prior's table but beside the prior at meals.[52] He appears to have had a taste for luxury and for high culture: despite being a cleric, the three books listed in his possession when his goods were seized in 1326 consisted of one bible and two romances – *Le Roman de la Rose* and a copy of the story of the grail.[53] He was the illegitimate son of a deacon[54] sent over from England by the king and listed as a baron in 1309.[55] By 1310 he was made escheator[56] and appears to have ensconced himself very early on in the tightly knit world of the local ecclesiastics, being granted the lands at Clonmethan near Swords in 1314.[57] Initially, he appears to have been closely associated with John de Hothum, acting as his attorney when Hothum returned to England.[58] But by the period 1317–19 there were a number of rather sharp rebukes from Hothum commanding him to stay in the castle and keep only his own household there[59] and to repair the bell of the Dublin church, St Mary Le Dam's, as he has been ordered.[60] In his accounts as escheator, the official whose role was to assess the value of lands coming into the king's hands and collect revenue from them, it can be seen that Islep managed, through some creative accounting, to ensure that the king owed him money by the end of his account.[61] Despite these irregularities, he managed to hold onto the position of treasurer for the periods 1314, when he took over from Bicknor until 1321 (nominating Outlaw as deputy treasurer during his trip to England in 1318) and 1322–5.[62] He worked hard at keeping in with the monarchy, sending the king a gift of a hobby horse and a dog in 1319.[63] During this period he was also granted an annual pension from the Dublin Augustinian house of All Hallows for advice to the prior.[64] But by 1321 he had to make the journey to England to account for his time as treasurer[65] and John Cogan took over the office.[66] He seems to have been able to give a satisfactory account of his activities for he was returned to the office of treasurer in 1322, with rights to dispose of lands without the interference of the then justiciar, John de Bermingham.[67] However, accusations of improper behaviour on his part continued to be sent to the King, including complaints from merchants in Chester and the burgesses of Cork.[68] By 1325 he was given respite from rendering his account as he was busy on the king's business[69] but later that year he was in prison, though just about to be released on having found sufficient guarantors to vouch for him.[70] John Darcy, the justiciar and Adam de Herwynton, a baron of the exchequer, were commanded to hold his goods.[71]

Adam de Herwynton is listed as the new treasurer[72] and from this point on, Islep's recorded career is made up of references to the on-going dispute as to his debts, in particular what he owed or did not owe the king. He was pardoned for sealing Bicknor's treasury rolls 'which contained many falsities' in 1326,[73] with a fine of 500 marks, but further charges of irregularities continued to be brought against him, notably by Reginald de Staunton, who brought a suit connected with the payment of the liberties of Trim.[74] Walter himself pleaded to the king that although he had paid 300 of the 500 mark fine, the administration in Dublin have seized his goods and refused him access to his lands.[75] At one stage he is listed as owing £753.3s. 6¼d. 'for divers concealments' and his land and goods are valued at £1,332. 18s. 1¼d.[76] Although Islep is recorded as being in England in 1329,[77] he must have kept his interest in Ireland if the dates of his corrodies at Kilmainham are taken into account, as he is listed as a corrody holder during the chapters of 1335, 1338 and 1339. In 1342 his lands were still being held by the king in consideration of the debts he owed.[78] Islep's career is interesting as an extreme case of a typical political career of the time, encompassing periods of disgrace and even imprisonment along with immense power and golden opportunities for personal advancement. His close association with and protection of the one-time treasurer Alexander Bicknor, who granted him the prebendary of Swords[79] in St Patrick's cathedral links him with a prelate whose career was even more tumultuous than Islep's own, encompassing accusations of heresy,[80] excommunication,[81] habitual debt[82] and the forging of the king's accounts.[83] The undeniably shady aspects of Bicknor's and Islep's political and administrative activities cast a revealing light on the community of which Outlaw was a part. As he acted as Islep's deputy during the two periods Islep was away from Ireland Outlaw must have been aware of the irregularities in the accounts. Yet he seemed to have had no difficulty in remaining close to him despite Islep's questionable financial integrity. Indeed, the magnificence of the corrodies granted to Islep and the very telling insistence that he be allowed to move his belongings freely in and out, suggest a possible role for Kilmainham as a safe house for the goods of those who did not want their possessions easily accessible to the king's officers. These corrodies were granted during the period when Islep was under constant threat of having all his goods taken from him by officials of the king for his past misdemeanours. Yet Outlaw, who set up the corrodies, was himself an official of the king and very much a part of the establishment. Is this a clear case of local loyalties superseding loyalty to the crown or the administration? Or a simple illustration of Outlaw's essentially self-interested and pragmatic approach, the action of a man who has no problem with acquiring advantages for his order at the cost of his loyalty as chancellor? The government sources, produced by the king's officials, can only present a bald statement of events and give little or no insight into the motivation of those involved in the convoluted play of shifting allegiances – but the events here seem to indicate a clear conflict of interests between loyalty to the monarch and loyalty to a local associate. In situations such as these, individuals such as Outlaw seem to have been able to operate in a dichotomous way, suffering no crisis of conscience from the fact that they might be involved in embezzling the king's finances on the one hand and fighting for him on the other. It is only fair to add that the king himself seems to have been capable of a similar kind of pragmatic mental dichotomy: during the period when Bicknor's financial affairs were under heavy investigation Edward III appealed to the pope to allow him to take counsel with the archbishop on secular matters, despite the fact that the archbishop was an excommunicate.[84] A further element in the on-going connection between Outlaw and Bicknor and Islep is the fact that they both come across as powerful and persuasive personalities, and in such a small, closed world, the importance of these factors cannot be underestimated.

With the exception of John de Hothum, Walter de Islep was possibly the most important of the corrody holders at Kilmainham, but there were many lesser officials who also availed of the lavish hospitality of the manor. One of these, John de Grauntsete was a justice of the bench in Dublin, who lost his position for a period for his illegal interference in a case between William of London and Walter de Islep.[85] De Grauntsete took William of London's side against Islep, which indicates that those who lodged together at Kilmainham did not necessarily side with each other in all matters. He was imprisoned but later released on payment of a fine (which he was pardoned from paying at a later date) and seems to have served the crown faithfully for many years. He was also deeply involved in the development of the city of Dublin itself: he married Alicia, daughter of Geoffrey de Mortone,[86] and through the years is listed as being engaged in various building works and land-holding schemes in the city. On occasion he acted as a messenger to the king in England[87] and was also involved in campaigns against the Irish, as the loss of his horse in one such campaign in 1334 indicates.[88] In later years he was granted the custody of the manor of Leixlip.[89] He and his wife Alicia de Morton – who was herself the daughter of a former lord mayor and notable builder – were involved in chapel building and had regular prayers and masses offered for their souls.[90] His corrodies at Kilmainham date from 1338 and 1339, but he appears to have been still active in Dublin in 1349 and even later, if the references to John de

Grauntsete are to himself and not to a son of the same name. Other prominent Dublin officials such as William le Mareschal, the brother of Brother John le Mareschal was also a holder of a valuable corrody at Kilmainham.

Among the other justices who lodged at Kilmainham was Walter de Kynefare who was active during the period 1323 to 1338. He was a secretary in the king's service and was paid expenses for his part in Outlaw's Munster campaign against Brian O' Brien.[91] A further group of corrodians, variously described as attorneys, record keepers, king's serjeants and keepers of the rolls include William de Boseworth,[92] William de Wideworth[93] and William de Bardelby.[94] De Bardelby is recorded as John de Hothum's deputy in Ireland in 1332. So also was Hugh de Nassyngton,[95] who is granted a generous corrody at Kilmainham with his wife Cecilia and was an official in the exchequer from at least 1327, when he was ordered to pay wages to Outlaw.[96] John de Hothum, onetime justiciar and bishop of Ely, who held a valuable corrody at Kilmainham does not appear to have availed greatly of his entitlement to lodge there.[97] Some corrodians were also granted tenancy of Hospitaller land, for example William de Wideworth who was given a lease on a messuage in Thomas Street.[98] The plethora of such grants to the record keepers and controllers of the purse strings of the Dublin exchequer gives a clear picture of the importance of the corrody system in Outlaw's mode of operation. The payment made or service given in the Kilmainham corrodies is rarely specified: but if these men had control of payments out of the exchequer and of the all-important records which acted as the sole arbitrator of rights and privileges, it is evident that they were in an ideal position to provide some recompense for their right to lodge at the manor. From the records which exist, it is not possible to establish whether Outlaw, as chancellor and on many occasions acting justiciar, may have been directly responsible for the appointment of some of these particular individuals to important positions in the administration: but there is ample evidence that once they were appointed Outlaw managed to create and maintain strong personal connections with them.

In addition to Outlaw's affiliation with those involved in the administration of the state, he also managed to connect to certain key members of the ecclesiastical establishment. The important contacts with Islep and Bicknor have already been discussed. Lesser clerics were also granted corrodies at the manor and were therefore drawn into the same circle. Some members of the Hospitaller order itself were active as members of the administration, such as Adam de Moure, listed as a clerk in 1316[99] and John de la Bataille, the witness to many of the Kilmainham grants, who is listed as keeper of writs and rolls of the Dublin bench in 1327[100] and acted as deputy to Prior Larcher as keeper of the seal for the period August to November 1342.[101] Religious connections to those outside the order can be seen in the provision of a corrody to Hugh de Saltu, a canon of St Patrick's, – he is recorded as being 'skilled in the law' in the papal letters of 1335[102] and is very possibly the same Hugh the Clerk listed as a witness with William Le Mareschal to a deed in 1320.[103] Another cleric and corrody holder was John de Horewode, archdeacon of Ossory[104] and granter of the manor of Lestronan in mortmain to Outlaw in 1338.[105] John de Horewode is himself listed as a tenant of the Hospitallers for land at Rathnaues.[106]

During his career, Outlaw demonstrated a profound knowledge of the local scene and what almost amounts to a genius for availing of opportunities to advance himself and his order. This involved close contact with individuals who were less than ethically pristine. However, it is important to see the members of his circle in the context of their time. The political climate of the first half of the fourteenth century was one of insecurity with an endemic threat of violence from all sides: from the Scots, from the Gaelic and from the feuds of the Anglo-Irish lords. In a frontier society someone who was a powerful magnate one day could end up a hostage, or worse, the day after. Even the monarchy was not stable: during Outlaw's career a king was deposed and murdered. It was a time of disorder and confusion, and of swiftly changing loyalties. Lands originally belonging to the colony were being devastated through war and famine, a situation which not only decreased crown revenues but provided a pretext for the unscrupulous to claim rights to these revenues or assert that the land was laid waste and the revenues gone. In the *Registrum* there is an interesting entry which indicates that even within the Hospitallers ecclesiastical tenants took advantage of the disturbances of the time to claim exemption from monies due to the order. The entry for William Crok specifies that while the money due from his rectory at Kilneynagh will be reduced if there is wastage or depopulation as a result of attacks from the Irish, such wastage must not be the result of William's own machinations.[107]

Given the devastation caused by on-going famine, the Bruce wars and the lands lost to the Irish, it is unsurprising that revenues due to the crown from Ireland fell sharply during the first quarter of the fourteenth century. Those in the very visible position of treasurer would be put under extra pressure and the returns from Ireland placed under exceptionally harsh scrutiny by the crown and the administration in England, particularly as this was also a time when English kings were in desperate need of finance for their own wars. Throughout the records, there are constant complaints of the arrears treasurers have fallen into. However, it does appear that Bicknor and Islep were either more acquisitive or dishonest than was the norm. It is useful to look at Outlaw's close association with them in the context of Robin Frame's analysis of relationships in the colony as a whole. Though referring to the alliances between the Anglo-Irish lords and their Gaelic neighbours, it could equally be applied to Outlaw's political associates: 'If we are to make sense of Anglo-

Ireland we must begin to see the building of local lordships, the formation of unconventional relationships, and the adjustments of attitudes as the necessary and positive things they were.'[108]

These relationships, whether positive or not, were very definitely necessary; survival in the political world of medieval Dublin would have been impossible without the ability to form such alliances. Outlaw developed an extremely efficient way to cement the connections necessary for survival and advancement. By literally bringing a large number of powerful men under the same roof at the safe haven at Kilmainham he not only rewarded their service to him but also increased their feeling of common identity. Within the confines of the manor he managed to create a community with himself at its centre. This must have acted as a very powerful force in upholding his position in the political life of the day and preventing the attempts to pry him loose from his place in the administration of Ireland. The various officials sent fresh from England to try to sort out the morass of local loyalties and in-fighting appear to have learnt very quickly to accept his position and co-operate with him. And Outlaw, despite the fact that he undoubtedly took advantage of the reigning confusion to acquire lands for his order, and his connections with particular individuals who may have put self-interest above their loyalty to the monarch, seems to have managed to hold onto an essential loyalty to the status quo. He was never recorded as being involved in any plots to overthrow the monarch, although the times he lived in would have given him ample opportunity to do so. In addition, at no time during his career does Outlaw himself seem to have been placed under investigation for dishonest dealings, in spite of having held the exposed post of treasurer. His connections with the record-keepers of the day might have something to do with this. Despite this, his position was doubtlessly extremely difficult at times, given the conflicting pressures he was under: he had to demonstrate loyalty to king, to his social network in Dublin, to the local administration, to the powerful lords he dealt with as chancellor and deputy justiciar, to his order, to the pope and finally, but possibly most importantly, to the small community of Hospitallers in Ireland. To retain the goodwill of all, he had to be an adept diplomat, and the description of the Franciscan chronicler Friar Clyn of Outlaw as a prudent and gracious man bears this out.[109] He demonstrated this graciousness in the provision of generous corrodies and lavish feasts at Kilmainham.

One English visitor, however, remained impervious to Outlaw's graciousness and diplomatic skills. This was Richard Ledrede, bishop of Ossory, who put forward what were probably the most damaging accusations of Outlaw's career. Ledrede's attempts to challenge those who controlled the small, tight nucleus of power in the colony came midway through Outlaw's political career and hit at those at the very heart of his circle.

# Outlaw and the Kyteler witchcraft case

The situation which brought Ledrede and Outlaw into conflict is now known as the Kilkenny witchcraft trial. The affair itself is a complicated one, and many different interpretations have been placed on the convoluted sequence of events surrounding the accusations made by Ledrede against a group of Kilkenny citizens in 1324. It has been variously interpreted as an expression of feuding between Anglo-Irish magnates,[1] a local symptom of the Mortimer/Despenser conflict,[2] a desperate fight against the forces of the ungodly[3] and a precursor of the great witch-hunts of the sixteenth century.[4] There were elements of all these aspects in the situation: but in addition to these it also arose as a result of violent personality clashes and power struggles between specific individuals. In common with the operations of any community, it contained local elements but was also a reflection of wider forces. As in any community drama the nature of the personalities involved had a significant influence on the course of the proceedings. Many of the roots of the affair lie in the personalities of the main players: Richard Ledrede, Arnold le Poer and Roger Outlaw. Roger Outlaw's role is rather more central than has often been acknowledged. While a large amount of recent interpretative material, such as the two articles by Neary,[5] is available, Outlaw's important role in the development of events has often been underplayed. A recent article by James Brennan[6] does not mention him at all. Although he was drawn into the matter in his role as chancellor, Outlaw would no doubt have become involved in any case because of his kinship to one of the accused, William Outlaw. The Kytéler witchcraft trial and the ensuing accusations by the bishop of Ossory constitute the major threat to Outlaw in his career as both government official and prior of the Hospital, but in addition it presents a clear example of the prior's *modus operandi* when confronted with opposition.

There are major problems in establishing the truth of exactly what happened during the Kyteler trial – or rather the series of trials and confrontations. This is because the main source for the trial, a document available in print under the title *A contemporary narrative of the proceedings against Dame Alice Kyteler*[7] (hereafter referred to as the *Narrative*) – was either written for, or very probably by the main player in the affair, the bishop of Ossory himself. The tone of the *Narrative* therefore portrays the bishop as the hero of the piece: he is given all the best lines and is constantly seen as triumphing over his adversaries. But despite its bias the *Narrative* is invaluable as a source on Outlaw and his community as it moves beyond the dry court records in helping us understand the motivations and loyalties behind the actions of those involved.

The trial and the events surrounding it make up a convoluted history, with accusation and counter-accusation flying between the bishop and his opponents. The style of the *Narrative* is baroque, involved and dramatic, at times histrionic. Much of the text is made up of the monologues of the bishop on his rights as an ecclesiastic, and the general rights and respect due to the church by the secular authorities. To understand the tone and preoccupations of the *Narrative* it is useful to look at the history and character of the bishop of Ossory.

Richard Ledrede was an Englishman who appears to have had no connection to Ireland or the colony when he was consecrated bishop of Ossory in 1317.[8] The appointment was a papal rather than a royal appointment and Ledrede does not appear to have had much influence with or connections to the English court. The new bishop entered into his duties with enthusiasm, for within a few weeks of taking up his place he had held a synod in Kilkenny.[9] One of the later articles in the synod as it is now recorded is a mandate against heretics, although Anne Neary argues that this article was an addition made after the Kyteler affair.[10] Ledrede was a Franciscan and had been consecrated at the court of Pope John XXII – a pope who was particularly concerned with the workings of magic and heresy. His papal bull *Super illus specula*[11] was the first to list sorcery as a form of heresy. Ledrede was a contemporary of the more famous Jacques Fournier, the bishop who later became Pope Benedict XII but at this point in time was heavily involved in the Cather inquisition at Montaillou, which effectively brought a whole village to trial for heresy.[12] Some years earlier the powerful Knights Templars had been destroyed by the accusations of heresy and witchcraft made by the French king. Coming from this background Ledrede would have been very aware of the possible threat of heresy – indeed, from the evidence of the Kilkenny case and his later career, it seems likely that he wished to set up an inquisition in Ireland.[13] There was resistance to such an approach in the English court, but nonetheless there were accusations of witchcraft made in court circles. One such is Despenser's complaint to the pope in 1324[14] that he is being threatened by magical and secret dealings. Belief in and fear of *maleficia* was a genuine concern of the time: both charms[15] and curses were seen as real forms of power. Ledrede himself calls down a lengthy and violent curse on those who ignore the dictates of his synod.[16] However, an accusation of witchcraft could also be a useful way of discrediting enemies. Ledrede was a man who wished to make his mark and he may not have been overly pleased to have been given a diocese which was a relative backwater in European terms. His personality – histrionic, obstinate and obsessive, would not have allowed him to fit easily into any society. He had no connections with the native Irish and he was seen as an outsider in the closely-knit community of Anglo-Norman Ireland, as Arnold le Poer's description of him as a 'vile rustic vagabond from England' demonstrates.[17] Despite the constant references in the *Narrative* to the support of the Franciscans, Dominicans and the ordinary people of Kilkenny, none are named: throughout the text the bishop appears as a solitary figure. The *Narrative* states that in the whole of Ireland there was not one to be found who dared or wished to publicly resist his opponents.[18] While this may be partly because the narrator wished to portray the bishop as an heroic figure taking on the on the powers of evil alone it may also be because there were few individual defenders of his position. His obsession with the secret plots of his enemies almost amounts to paranoia. He appears to have never managed to integrate into the colony, being forced into exile from his diocese for much of his later life.

Ledrede appears to have run into problems with the local administration early on in his career, as a papal letter 1320 indicates.[19] Given his love of drama and pre-occupation with heresy the complaint of witchcraft and heresy on the part of their step-mother put before him by Alice Kyteler's step-children was positively providential, giving him the opportunity to uncover a nest of evil heretics in his diocese. Briefly, the story commences with the accusation that Dame Alice had enchanted and murdered her three previous husbands and had acquired their goods for herself and the son of her first marriage, William Outlaw. Her present husband, John de Poer, was currently suffering from a sickness which made his hair and nails fall out and on investigation of Alice's rooms had discovered a chest full of the paraphernalia of witchcraft.[20]

Alice is the most enigmatic figure in the whole affair: it is unlikely that such accusations could be made without some evidence, and the symptoms of her husband bear a close resemblance to those of someone suffering from arsenic poisoning. In addition there is evidence that Alice did manage to have goods made over to herself and her son by her previous husbands. However, it is also true that as banker and a money-lender she may have been a target for envy and antagonism in the town of Kilkenny. Money plays a significant role in the sequence of events – it is the initial reason for the accusations made and may also be one of the reasons why the prior of the Hospitallers was so eager to protect his rich Kilkenny relatives. William Outlaw was rich enough to act as a money-lender to Edward II – he is one of a list of magnates the king appeals to for financial help in 1322.[21]

It is unnecessary to subscribe to the wilder theories of feminist history to see in Alice a woman who had very definitely stuck her head above the parapet: she was both economically powerful and sexually active. This combination certainly also affected the depth of the reforming bishop's response to her and his obsessive pursuit of her downfall. Ledrede was so offended by the bawdy songs sung by those living in his diocese that he had written hymns to be sung to the same tunes.[22] He appears to have had a particular attachment to the figure of the Virgin Mary. (One of the conditions of the penance the bishop eventually inflicted on William Outlaw was for him to have masses offered before a statue of the Virgin Mary, which the bishop was to have made and painted.) In this context it is easy to see the emotional force of the opposition between the figure of the pure young virgin feeding her child milk (a frequent symbol in Ledrede's poems) and the evil old woman feeding her husband poison. The emphasis on the sexual nature of the relationship between Alice and her demon, Robin Artisson, is the first case of such an accusation in the history of European witchcraft.[23] Psychological studies of the phenomenon of the witch-hunt have put forward the argument that the identification of an evil figure in the community can act as a projection of all the unacknowledged and anti-social desires and impulses of the individuals who make up the community.[24] Robin Briggs, in a study of witchcraft in early modern France speaks of the 'theatres of the mind' where this conflict between good and evil is enacted and 'dramas of deep personal significance are repeatedly played out.'[25]

Whatever his motivation, from the beginning of the affair Ledrede displayed an obsessive need to bring about the downfall and public humiliation of Dame Alice and her supporters, seeing in them a highly organised and powerful sect of heretics and witches. He acted quickly on the accusations, excommunicating Alice and contacting the Dublin authorities with a request to have her arrested for heresy. It is at this point that Roger Outlaw enters the story, for as acting justiciar in place of the absent John Darcy, he had responsibility to expedite the warrant. Outlaw is described as a kinsman of William Outlaw in the *Narrative*[26] and from the beginning he protected Dame Alice and her son from the bishop, taking refuge in the letter of the law to do so. He claimed that he could not arrest Alice until the warrant had been served for forty days. When Ledrede then called Alice to appear before him as her bishop, she fled to Dublin and apparently took refuge with Outlaw, for he sent representation for her to the bishop's court. Ledrede then called her son William to appear before him, but in the meantime, William had been in contact with the seneschal of Kilkenny, Arnold le Poer, who attempted without success to persuade the bishop to drop the action. In an ill-judged move, le Poer had the bishop arrested and thrown into prison until the time when William was to due to appear before him had passed. The *Narrative* makes great drama from the arrest and imprisonment of the bishop, who on his release insisted on being dressed in his full pontificals as he made his way through a great crowd of people. He continued in his relentless pursuit of William Outlaw, again citing him to appear before him, but was then called to Dublin by Outlaw as chancellor and William Rodeyard, dean of St. Patrick's and acting in the absence of the archbishop of Dublin, (Archbishop Bicknor was in England at this period) to answer charges as to why he had placed the diocese of Ossory under an interdict. The bishop refused to go, but was later compelled to make his way to Dublin to answer the appeal of Kyteler against the charges of heresy and at Roger Outlaw's instigation, to answer to parliament. By this stage Outlaw had made it amply plain where his loyalties lay and is perhaps one of the 'enemies' which the *Narrative* claims planned an ambush against Ledrede on his way to Dublin – an ambush the bishop avoided by taking a circuitous and savage route.[27] The account makes much of Ledrede's appearance before the Dublin parliament, where he put forward a spirited defence of his dignity as an ecclesiastic and the rights of the spiritual over the temporal.[28] Le Poer was forced to beg pardon for imprisoning the bishop – the bishop had the warrant to prove it – and it was agreed that the heretics should be pursued, but despite this apparent resolution the affair was not yet over, for Ledrede was unable to obtain the papers for the arrest of Alice from Roger Outlaw, whose responsibility it was to produce them. Here it is obvious that Outlaw was using a bureaucratic go-slow to stall the bishop, as he had used the letter of the law to prevent Alice's original arrest. Ledrede persisted and Lady Alice fled: later chronicles say that she went to England. Ledrede appealed to the justiciar, John Darcy, who eventually had warrants made out for the arrest of the accused which included Alice, William and ten other accomplices. The affair then seems to have entered into a (probably deliberate) bureaucratic morass as some of those arrested were released on sureties and the administration claimed it could not re-arrest them. Arnold le Poer's threat to the bishop,[29] made in the early days of the trial, that he would be obstructed at every turn is clearly being fulfilled and the *Narrative* complains of the 'skilled legal experts' ranged against Ledrede.[30] Eventually, however, William appeared before the bishop in Kilkenny and submitted to him. On the supplication of the chancellor and treasurer he had his prison sentence commuted to a penance which included roofing Kilkenny cathedral in lead. He apparently did not hold to the conditions of his penance and was again brought before Ledrede in January 1325. In the meantime, the other 'witches' were arrested and one, Petronilla of Meath, Alice's servant, was flogged until she confessed. She was burnt at the stake in November 1324.[31] At the January trial of William Outlaw, Roger agreed to act as guarantor for his kinsman's compliance with the conditions of his penance, and also to supply the bishop with the fruits of the church at Gowran in Kilkenny, which had originally been a Templar foundation but for which the Hospitallers had acquired the rights.[32] Petronilla de Midia, without the connections or wealth of William Outlaw, was the only one of the twelve named heretics to die as a result of Ledrede's persecution.

Outlaw's behaviour throughout the affair demonstrates a great loyalty to his kin and to his circle, while at the same time showing a shrewd ability to gauge the possibility of victory or the need for compromise. The relationship between Ledrede and himself is interesting, not least because they appear to be completely opposite in their personalities and modes of operation. Ledrede considered that once he had right (and Church law) on his side he was justified in his actions, however extreme. Outlaw was a diplomat, seeking ways around problems in the letter of the law, but also prepared to discuss and bargain. John Watt sees the *Narrative* as essentially an account of how members of the Irish administration (i.e. Outlaw and le Poer) resisted Ledrede's attempts to have the secular powers act as the police force of ecclesiastical authority in pursuing the accused.[33] While Outlaw, unlike his friend Arnold le Poer, used reasoned argument rather than outright force and in the main was careful to try to keep his position of chancellor look unblemished by violence against the church, it could not be claimed that he gave the impression of neutrality. During the height of the affair he and Walter de Islep (described in the *Narrative* as a friend of le Poer)[34] stayed in William Outlaw's house in Kilkenny – thus proclaiming his loyalty in the most obvious way. At the final trial of William Outlaw Ledrede berated the chancellor for this action. In a remarkable tirade the bishop recited a litany of Outlaw's misdemeanours, and threatened to have the pope himself denounce the chancellor if he did not take on the task of combating heresy. Ledrede also made angry references to the fact that the chancellor has tried to block him at every step and that he is aware of 'how well you know us and can hurt us and oppress us.'[35] The *Narrative* states that Outlaw was so overcome by the bishop's eloquence that he 'burst into tears'[36] and acknowledged his fault, claiming that these mistakes were made through ignorance, not malice. This picture of the hard-headed campaigner and shrewd politician crying on the stand is hard to accept at face value. In the light of his later actions it is extremely unlikely that Outlaw was overcome with remorse: so it may be that these public tears are a fabrication – that this incident has been added to the narrative because it is what the bishop would have liked to have happened rather than what actually took place. It is also possible that Outlaw was playing the role of penitent in order to appease the bishop's need for drama. The bargain which was struck between the bishop and Outlaw had more to do with hard cash than real contrition, but a scene involving an admission of guilt may have been necessary to Ledrede to maintain his self-image as an incorruptible. This public humiliation may therefore have been a part of the price the Outlaw family had to pay. Despite the bishop's harangue, Outlaw did not oblige the bishop in his request that the chancellor take an oath binding the administration to take action against those accused of heresy by a bishop. Ledrede's victory was not, therefore, fully complete.

Given the style of the narrative, the Kyteler affair can sometimes appear in the light of farce, but the seriousness of the charges of heresy levied against

the accused of 1324 and later against Roger Outlaw and Arnold le Poer should
not be underestimated. Outlaw seems to have avoided further confrontation
with the bishop for a four-year period. The earl of Kildare, who was justiciar
in 1328, complained to the king that Outlaw was too busy to give assistance
in investigating his accusations against Ledrede and hints that Outlaw was in
collusion with the bishop.[37] But late in this same year Ledrede accused both
the chancellor and le Poer (who had just returned from England) of protecting
heretics, and in the case of le Poer, attacking Ossory churches.[38] The enmity
between le Poer and Ledrede seems to have continued unabated between 1325
and 1328 and Ledrede's actions suggest an enmity to the whole le Poer family.
As late as 1355 he was cited as being involved in an attack on one of the le
Poers.[39] In the endemic feuding of the late twenties and early thirties, Kildare,
de Burgh and the le Poers were in opposition to the Butlers, Berminghams
and Desmonds of Munster, in a local conflict which some historians have
claimed found expression in the polarisation of support in the Despenser/
Mortimer conflict.[40] Accusations were also made at the time that the earl of
Desmond was in collusion with the Irish Brian O'Brien. Ledrede's loyalty was
definitely on the side of the earl of Desmond and he is cited one of those
present at the secret meeting held in Kilkenny which vowed to put the earl of
Desmond on the throne of Ireland. The authenticity of this accusation has
been questioned,[41] as it bears the marks of a plan to discredit the individuals
alleged to be involved; but the fact that such an accusation could be made
indicates where Ledrede's sympathies were seen to lie. There is even a
suggestion that the religious houses may have been involved in taking sides in
this dispute. In a discussion of an early fourteenth-century manuscript held at
the Hospitaller house of Kilbarry in Waterford, which records the death of a
le Poer (Cambridge, Corpus Christi MS 405) Evelyn Mullally compares it to
the British Library Harley MS 913, (which includes a copy of the songs
written by the earl of Desmond) and concludes:

> While it would be quite unjustified to talk of literary patronage, Corpus
> Christi 405 was probably assembled in a milieu sympathetic to the Le
> Poers, just as Harley 913 was probably produced in a milieu sympathetic
> to the Earl of Desmond. Corpus Christi 405 was owned by a house of
> the Hospitallers, while Harley 913 has connections with the
> Franciscans.[42]

While I can find no other evidence of enmity between the Franciscans and
the Hospitallers (indeed, Clyn, a Franciscan from Kilkenny, does not appear to
have been a supporter of Ledrede and speaks highly of Outlaw) it is more than
possible that Ledrede's resentment of Outlaw was increased by the
Hospitallers' close and on-going connection with the le Poers. He would also

have deeply resented the fact that the Hospitallers did not answer to episcopal authority but directly to the pope.

Ledrede attempted to gain an even greater victory over le Poer and Roger Outlaw in 1328 when he brought accusations of heresy against them both. Outlaw attempted to help le Poer fight the charges but in 1329 the seneschal died in Dublin Castle, awaiting trial.[43] Outlaw managed to clear himself of the accusations of heresy made by Ledrede: he called a parliament and invited charges to be brought against him. A jury made up of local ecclesiastics and magistrates then gave judgement on his case. He was able to call on the most important churchmen in the city; William Rodeyard, who was acting in place of the absent Archbishop Bicknor, the priors of St Mary's, St Thomas and Holy Trinity and two justices, Elias Lawless and Peter Willeby.[44] He was cleared of any taint of heresy, and according to the Dublin annalist held a great feast to celebrate his victory.[45] The personality of Arnold le Poer himself is perhaps one of the reasons the case was taken so far and also gives some indication of the arrogant pride of some of the colonial families. Le Poer was a brave soldier but he was also violent and impetuous, and had an uncontrolled tongue. He was clearly incensed that some low-born outsider should come to Ireland which he claims was known for its holiness – and with his papal bulls and rules no-one has ever heard off, accuse the natives of heresy.[46] His impulsive nature led him to engage in such acts as man-handling Ledrede when the bishop had carefully worn the communion host on his body so that le Poer could be accused of attacking the body of Christ.[47] If le Poer's behaviour is compared with that of Outlaw, we can see the reason why the affair ended with Outlaw feasting with his friends, while le Poer's body was left lying unburied for days after his death because of his excommunicate status.[48]

The accusation of heresy made against Outlaw was undoubtedly the most important personal threat to him during his career. Burnings for heresy were rare in Ireland[49] and England at this period and while it is unlikely that Outlaw, given his connections, would have suffered the same fate as the unfortunate Petronilla, he would have been very conscious of the potential of loss to himself and his order through these accusations. The possessions of heretics were automatically forfeit and the Templar trials had taken place only ten years earlier, after which that order had lost all its lands and wealth. These circumstances would have been still fresh in the mind of Outlaw, the head of the order which had profited so greatly from the Templar losses. It is interesting that one of the charges against William was the very specific charge that he wore the devil's girdle on his body – exactly the same charge that had been levied against the Templars.[50] Outlaw earned the enmity of Ledrede through his support of Kyteler and William Outlaw, having used his position, his knowledge of and skill in the law and finally his wealth in an attempt to protect them: an attempt which was at least partially effective. The methods he

4. Tombstone of Richard Ledrede in St Canice's Cathederal, Kilkenny.
(Photograph Maura Leahy)

used – blocking and stalling, ignoring warrants, making counter-accusations which confused the issue to such an extent that those involved were in danger of forgetting the original charges – are the weapons of the politician and the bureaucrat and give a good indication of the type of power Outlaw had at his disposal in the administration. They may even provide one key as to why Outlaw was able to hold to his position as chancellor despite the attempts to replace him – if his Kilmainham lodgers used the same tactics against an outsider in their roles in the administration it would have been impossible for the bureaucracy to function. One can also see how such an affair could strengthen the links between Outlaw and someone such as Walter de Islep who supported him in his efforts.

Despite the somewhat circumscribed victory Ledrede achieved in the Kyteler case, he never became a powerful figure in the colony: indeed he spent much of his episcopate in exile abroad. Within a few years of taking up his position as bishop, he had managed to make enemies of many important individuals in the colony. De Burgh, justiciar in 1328, wrote claiming that Ledrede had accused Queen Isabella of sorcery.[51] He also incurred the enmity of Alexander Bicknor, who was also accused by Ledrede of harbouring heretics in later years and who in turn accused Ledrede of heresy.[52] The feud between them continued right up to the time of Bicknor's death. In 1329 Ledrede was called to answer charges of heresy in Dublin, and claiming to fear for his life, he sailed in secret for Avignon where he was to remain for nine years. From this point on Outlaw managed to avoid overt conflict with Ledrede for after the collapse of the 1328 accusations Ledrede did not attempt to attack him directly again, and given Ledrede's long-term absence from his See, Outlaw did not bother to seek confrontation. The chancellor had weathered one of the most dangerous threats to his career and his time, taken up as it was with the '*bosoignes del hospital*'[53] was being more profitably spent than in locking horns with the over-fervent bishop of Ossory.

# The 'Legacy' of Outlaw?

If the public apology inflicted on Roger Outlaw by Richard Ledrede at Kilkenny and the later accusations of heresy against him may have been a source of embarrassment to the prior of the Hospitallers, they do not seem to have damaged his career in the long term. Soon after Outlaw was cleared of the charges of heresy, he held another great feast, this time to celebrate the peace that had been made at a Dublin parliament presided over by Outlaw. The earl of Ulster, the earl of Louth and the maverick Maurice Fitzthomas, the earl of Desmond were involved in this treaty, which must have been considered a diplomatic success for Outlaw, bringing together as it did some of the most bloody-minded of the magnates. Outlaw's celebration was one of the three great feasts were held – one in Dublin Castle presided over by the earl of Ulster, one in St Patrick's presided over by Maurice Fitzthomas and one in Kilmainham presided over by Outlaw.[1] Unfortunately, the peace they were celebrating did not last for very long.

Apart from two short periods – in 1331 and 1336 – Outlaw remained chancellor until the end of his life. During the period in 1331 when he was commanded to hand over the rolls to Adam de Lymberg, Outlaw visited the king, ostensibly to inform him of the state of the lordship but also no doubt to work on improving his own standing with the monarch. If this was the case, it appears to have been a success: Clyn mentions the special favour of the king in regard to Outlaw in his obituary of the prior. However, during the last years of his career cracks were beginning to show in his relationship with the king and the council in England. In 1333 a stern warning was addressed to the chancellor and the justiciar against taking 'divers royal prises of victuals and other things in the said land, for their benefit . . . to the great harm of the common people.'[2] These 'prises' were not legitimately owed, and a complaint of this behaviour on the part of his officials had come to the king's attention. While Outlaw's replacement as chancellor by the bishop of Hereford in 1336 lasted no more than a year it can be seen as a forerunner of Edward III's attempt to purge the administration in 1341.

From 1336 ordinances were passed attempting to control the activities of the Dublin officials. An order of June 1336 reads:

> Order to treat and judge all who ought to be ruled by the English law, in equal law, great and small, rich and poor . . . because it has been shown to the king by honest men of those parts and public fame

proclaims that the justiciary, chancellor and other ministers . . . show too
great a favour to the powerful, permitting them to oppress the poor, to
invade the king's rights . . . and perpetrate various crimes.[3]

Some officials were replaced by new men from England[4] and Thomas of
Hereford, brother to the new chancellor John Charlton, was sent to Ireland as
justiciar with specific instructions to reform the state of the lordship.[5] It is
possible that Outlaw, who must have been ageing at this period, may have
been finding it harder to contain the squabbles of the magnates and keep
public disorder at a level acceptable to the king. What Frame describes as the
'crisis' of 1341–2 developed very quickly in the year following Outlaw's death.
The immediate cause of the crisis was Edward III's revocation of grants made
to the Anglo-Irish, including the grants of Leixlip and Chapelizod to the
Hospitallers. This, and the introduction of more new officials from London
resulted in a total refusal of the Anglo-Irish to co-operate with the
government. They met in Kilkenny and produced a petition which they sent
to the king in late 1341. John Larcher, prior of the Hospitallers in Ireland acted
as one of the messengers. The petition complained of abuses by the
administration and required that a commission be set up to examine its
practices. Robin Frame sees this as an attempt to blame the ministers rather
than the king for their difficulties, and thus put forward protests about royal
policies without the king having to accept censure.[6] If this is so the ploy
worked: Edward III retracted the revocation and removed most of the new
officials, re-granting the Chapelizod and Leixlip lands to the Hospitallers and
appointing Larcher chancellor in early 1342. The status quo was upheld.
Larcher, an Englishman, had been sent to Ireland as prior by the grand master
in 1341. He replaced John le Mareschal who had been elected prior by his
confreres in Ireland directly after Outlaw's death.[7]

Larcher was close to the grand master and the centre of Hospitaller power.
No doubt he was more dedicated to the broader aims of the Hospitaller order
than Outlaw and had differing loyalties from him. Both within the Irish
section of the order and the Dublin administration Larcher would have been
considered an outsider, being English by birth and having spent long periods
in Rhodes.[8] It could have been no easy task to take control of the priory from
the hands of the powerful le Mareschal brothers who hold such a prominent
place in the records of the *Registrum*, but Larcher seems to have managed to
do this: there is no mention of John Le Mareschal's name on the witness list
of the 1348 chapter.[9] The fact that in 1341 – just a few months after his arrival
– he was entrusted to take the petition of the Anglo-Irish to the king indicates
that he managed to integrate into the community with astonishing rapidity.
He held the post of chancellor for a four month period in 1342 after which
John de la Bataille (also a member of the Hospitallers) acted as his deputy for

a short period – which indicates that he was again out of Ireland at this point.[10] It appeared possible that Larcher, prior and chancellor, would have a similar career to Outlaw. But this was not to be the case. Larcher held the post of chancellor until 1346 when he was replaced by John Darcy but he recovered his position in 1347 and held it until 1348. During this period he was also deputy justiciar, but in 1348 his name disappears from the records of the administration in Ireland.[11] By this time he had been replaced as prior of the order by John Tylloch. He appears to have died suddenly in 1349 – Otway-Ruthven suggests from plague.[12] Apart from Outlaw, Larcher was to be the longest serving Irish prior of the seven who took up important roles in the administration during the history of the Hospitallers in Ireland. Outlaw's predecessors, Prior William Fitzroger (deputy justiciar 1284–5) and Prior William of Rosse (deputy justiciar 1301–2) had held their posts for no more than a year. Prior John le Frowyk is listed as chancellor from 1356 to 1357 and again in 1359.[13] His successor Thomas Burley was removed from his post for fraud[14] and was later imprisoned by the Berminghams. William Tany acted as chancellor from 1372 to 1376 and was elected justiciar by the council in Ireland in 1373 but his appointment was rescinded by the king.[15] Several priors, including Frowyk and Burley,[16] were sent to England with petitions lamenting the state of the lordship and looking for assistance from the king in their struggle against Gaelic resurgence and internal feuds. Thus the Hospitallers continued to be considered a factor in the defence of the Anglo–Norman colony and identified with the official power of the Lordship – but the identification is no longer with a successfully functioning entity.

It is not only in comparison with other priors of Kilmainham that Outlaw's career appears exceptionally stable. Very few high-ranking officials of the time seem to have been able to keep their posts for long periods. In all, Outlaw was chancellor for almost twenty years. During this time there were no less than nine different individuals taking the post of justiciar or acting justiciar – some of these for extremely short periods. Even from 1329 when the position became more stable – John Darcy held the position for thirteen years – the titular chief governor was frequently absent and his post taken by a deputy. On eight occasions Outlaw was the deputy in question.[17] The post of treasurer was even more precarious: between 1322 and 1341 there were twelve different individuals listed as holding the position. Against this background Outlaw's ability to hold his own is obvious. The post of chancellor was, admittedly, somewhat more stable as prior to 1340 there were times when officers such as Thomas Quantock held the post for long periods. But this changed in the second half of the century – during the forty years after Outlaw's death there were no fewer than nineteen different chancellors, none serving more than six years and many of them serving for less than a year. In many cases the individuals served for a short period, are replaced by someone else and then come back into power. During the same period there were fourteen different chief governors and twenty-one treasurers.[18] It has been argued that it was difficult to find men of good calibre willing to take posts in the backwater of the Irish administration,[19] (a backwater that seemed to be gaining the reputation of being an extremely muddy one as regards official probity) and it may be that many of those who were removed from their posts – such as Robert de Pyncebek, chancellor of the exchequer in 1340[20] – were dismissed because of simple incompetence. Equally, it is possible that Edward III was

5. Fra Helion de Villeneuve, from *Statuta Hospitalis Hierusalem*, compiled by Friar Hugo. De Villeneuve was the grand master of the Hospitaller's during Outlaw's priorship.

unwilling to allow the kind of power base which the men of Outlaw's generation had developed evolve again. But the lack of any stability in these positions, particularly in the case of the post of chancellor, may be taken to at once demonstrate the increasing instability of the Lordship and to have intensified it.

It is not only in terms of his political career that Outlaw may be seen as an exception. His career in the Hospitaller order may also be contrasted with many other priors in relation to the length of time he retained his position as prior. He was confirmed in the office of prior by the General Chapter of 1331 for another ten years,[21] a confirmation which brought him to the end of his life. This re-election was by no means always automatic in the case of the Hospitallers: prior Thomas Larcher had been removed from the office of Grand Prior in England in 1328, because of ineptitude and senility.[22] Prior Walter del Aqua lived for a number of years after Outlaw took over as prior, as he is listed as a witness to the chapter of 1326, alive and well and living near Carrickfergus.[23]

In addition, none of the priors of Kilmainham in the later half of the fourteenth century seem to have continued Outlaw's achievement in combining success within their order and the administration: John Fitzrichard, the successor of Prior Larcher, supported Alexander Bicknor's unsuccessful party in the dispute over the Armagh primacy and died mysteriously soon after the issue was resolved – possibly also from the plague.[24] By 1363 Edward III still considered the Hospitaller order an important element in the defence of the colony, but he had ordered his officials in Ireland to investigate the order and the alienation of lands apparently taking place under John le Frowyk, stating: 'the maintenance of the brethren in Ireland, who hold a good position for the repulse of the King's Irish enemies is much impaired.'[25] Le Frowyk had brought the Hospital to such a state that the knights of Ireland were no longer in a position to send money to support the Hospitallers' battles in Rhodes and his successor William Tany is described as having further reduced the state of the Hospital.[26] In 1388, the prior of the time appears to have been running into problems with local debts as there is an entry in the first volume of the *Calendar of the ancient records of Dublin* which is includes an inventory of the goods and a list of debts owed to John Hamound, cobbler. The prior of Kilmainham is listed as owing him forty-six shillings, for boots and shoes. As we can estimate from other entries that one could get thirty pairs of shoes for ten shillings, the prior either had very expensive tastes and let his debts run up enormously, or the quantity of footwear required by the prior indicates a vast number of retainers. To put this in context, the prior of All Saints, another major religious house of the time, owed only twenty-two shillings. Perhaps the prior of the Kilmainham house was not a good client, for Hamound's will is also included and it appears that the cobbler left nothing to the brothers at

Kilmainham. In contrast he left large sums of money to a very long list of abbeys and churches – he almost seems to have included every religious house in Dublin with the exception of the Hospitallers. Hamound wished to be buried at Newgate, at the other Dublin Hospital of St John the Baptist run by the Crutched Priors, which was traditionally far more involved in the activities of caring for the sick and the poor.[27]

The decline towards disorder cannot, of course, be totally laid at the door of the individual priors: the colony in Ireland was itself in decline during the latter half of the fourteenth century and such major catastrophes as the Black Death would have played a major role in hastening this decline. By the beginning of the fifteenth century the Hospitallers in Ireland no longer operated as an efficient and unified army: there were on-going disputes and dissension and some, notably James Keating, became involved in local feuding when his anti-Tudor stance put the order in Ireland at risk.[28] In the latter half of the century there were increasing efforts from England to gain control of the Irish priory, mainly through the appointment of English priors – at the end of the fourteenth century, the Irish priory was refusing to recognise the appointment of the Englishman, Peter Holt.[29] Charles Tipton has argued that Outlaw's successful career may have been a reason for this increased interest: the Templar lands had made it 'a prize worth having.'[30] During the Great Schism the Irish priory under Prior Richard White supported the grand master of the order elected by the anti-pope, thus causing a split with the English *langue*.[31]

If we compare the situation of the Irish and English priories interesting contrasts appear. In structure and administration the two priories were similar: the same rule with its emphasis on rigid conformity and obedience followed and there was the same organisational system in place. For the purposes of comparison there is a useful Extent of 1338 which lists both income and expenditure in the houses of the order in England.[32] The order here was far larger and more widely spread, with 119 brothers, eighty corrodians and two donates listed.[33] The Irish priory paid only a quarter of the responsions payable by the English one.[34] It is not possible to ascertain with any reliability the number of professed knights and brothers in the Irish priory, but during the period of the *Registrum* corrodies were granted to 102 individuals. Twelve of these can be positively identified as brothers of the order, indicating that there may have been up to ninety corrodians in Ireland who were not members of the order at this time – more than in England, Scotland and Wales put together.[35] The same sources of income were available to the Irish and English brothers – farming, livestock, rents, milling, fishing and the benefices of the churches in their possession. They emphasised hospitality and operated the same corrody system, with some significant variations.[36] The layout and structure of the priory buildings appear to have been similar, including the presence of domestic apartments above the vault of the church.[37] The same rigid hierarchy of seating at mealtimes was observed. Smaller camerae such as Hampton in England appear to have operated on a similar basis to the smaller houses in Ireland with no more than two brothers in residence and the activity geared towards farming.[38] Finally, in areas such as Scotland and the marches of Wales the Hospitallers acted as defenders of the power of the Anglo-Norman kingship against native elements. But there were significant differences: physical distance from the crown and the English nobles gave the Hospitaller order in Ireland a freedom it could not possess in England. The English monarch felt free to regularly instruct the order in England to grant corrodies in reward for services done to the crown. There is no evidence of this ever having happened in Ireland – certainly during the period when Outlaw was prior. At the main house of the Hospitallers at Clerkenwell in London the king, his family and friends were regular and long-term visitors, as the nearest royal palace was outside the city. These extra expenditures of the English house seem to have been felt as a burden on the order and the subject of complaint on occasion.[39] But they do not explain the disorder and debt into which the priory in England fell during the priorship of Thomas Larcher. Leonard de Tibertis had been sent by the grand master to look into the affairs of the English house and found them in total chaos. Thomas Larcher was finally removed from his office because of incompetence, with the order owing huge amounts to money lenders from the Italian states.[40] An interesting reference to the Society of the Bardi of Florence in the Kilmainham *Registrum*[41] indicates that Outlaw also had dealings with Italian money-lenders at some point in his career. Larcher was eventually replaced by the highly efficient Philippus de Thame, who turned the affairs of the Hospital around and within ten years of Larcher's removal in 1328 it was again showing a healthy profit. Despite de Thames' evident probity and effectiveness, his list of expenses includes a large number of 'presents' to local officials: Kemble speculates that these were probably paid to assist the Hospitallers in the process of acquiring the Templar lands.[42] In England, the acquisition of the Templar property appears to have been something of a poisoned chalice, involving the order in lengthy and costly litigation – the lands here were much more extensive and much more accessible to the king than the Templar lands in Ireland. When the Hospitallers eventually acquired them the lands had often been devastated. One of the successes of Outlaw's career may be considered the way he managed to maintain steady progress in the acquisition of much of the Templar property during the period he was prior.

There is some evidence that there were problems of discipline and control generally in the Hospitaller order during the fourteenth century. The chapter general at Rhodes in 1344 contains admonitions against dainty food, silver plate, keeping many attendants and wearing costly and disorderly robes.[43]

However, such admonitions were regularly voiced throughout the history of the Hospitaller order and the secular nature of the orders' activities and involvements made such behaviour a common problem. The order seems to have been also particularly notable for the fine horses they rode – though given the extent of Outlaw's travels throughout Ireland an investment in a good horse would appear to have been sound common sense rather than a luxury.[44] What was a new and possibly catastrophic development for the order during the middle of the century was the advent of the Black Death. The order in general, like any concentration of population, must have suffered greatly from the on-going epidemics of the Black Death which in Ireland began in 1348, with large-scale local outbreaks to 1384. There is no documentation available on the direct effect of the Black Death on the Hospitaller order, but towns and monasteries where people were grouped together were the hardest hit by disease. Clyn claims that Dublin lost 14,000 people between August and December 1348.[45] While medieval chroniclers are notorious for their exaggeration of numbers, the scale of the disaster must have indeed been great to have given rise to such a figure.

Other external influences brought division to the Hospitaller order; the period of the Great Schism when part of the Hospitaller order supported the pope and part the anti-pope would also have played a part in spreading dissension and disunity.

On a specifically local level, there is some evidence to show that the Hospitaller house at Kilmainham began to decline almost directly after the death of Outlaw. The sources for the period after his death are limited and it is necessary to examine them with care: this is particularly the case with the Kilmainham *Registrum*. The *Registrum*, according to McNeill:

> was not a compilation but a *copy* from a continuous record already in existence. The remaining entries after Outlaw's date are written in a very small script, much inferior to that of the earlier portion; it may be concluded that they are a later addition crowded into the blank pages of a volume already made up.[46]

It is necessary to ask some questions here about the how the records were being kept. It is possible that the first part of the *Registrum*, which deals with grants and agreements during Outlaw's priorship, was made from existing documentation after his death – this would explain why all the entries are in the same hand. If this was the case, the copy may well have been made before the arrival of John Larcher from England and therefore open to some embellishment by John le Mareschal and the other inmates of Kilmainham at the time. He and some of his colleagues are certainly given very generous corrodies. However, such a possibility can only be speculated on, and it is safe

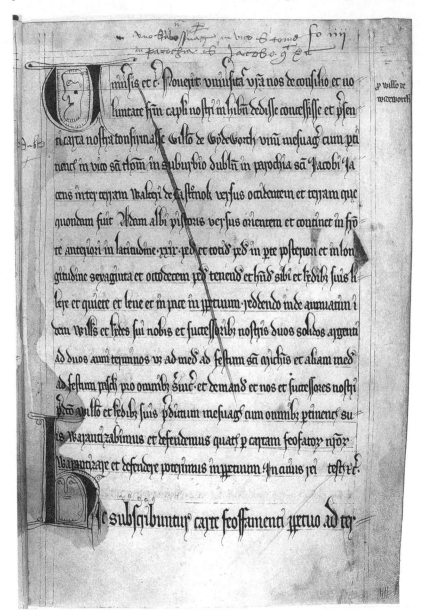

6. Folio 4 recto of Registrum de Kilmainham (Ms Rawlinson B501).
Note decorated capitals.

7. Folio 114 recto of Registrum de Kilmainham. (Ms Rawlinson B501), written after Outlaw's death. Note smaller, less ornate script.

to say from the other evidence which exists that the *Registrum* remains true to the tone of Outlaw's priorship. It is equally possible that Outlaw himself, concerned for his advancing years, was intent on copperfastening the position of friends such as Walter de Islep before his death and had the copy made as extra security. As early as 1333 Outlaw is securing his own position for the time when he will no longer be prior,[47] being confirmed in the lands at Kilsaran, Clontarf and the whole bailiwick of Ulster. He was certainly a shrewd enough individual to put his affairs in order and confirm grants to his supporters if he felt either his health or his power was under threat. Throughout the *Registrum* there are confirmations of grants which have been in operation for some time, and are simply being officially recorded and confirmed at a chapter.

The typical number of listings for the last years of Outlaw's priorship are thirty-three for the chapter of 1338[48] and twenty for the chapter of 1339.[49] The undated entries which follow directly after these, in different writing, are listed as having been confirmed under the priorship of John le Mareschal – all twenty-three of them, including an increase in provision for his brother William.[50] There is then a gap of at least seven years before the next chapter is recorded – a gap which in itself is significant. There are only ten transactions listed for this next chapter, which was held towards the end of Larcher's priorship in 1348. None of these corrodies are of a high level, mainly dealing with the appointment of servants.[51] The only corrody listed for Kilmainham is one for the chief cook. The listing for John Fitzrichard's chapter at Killergy in 1349 is longer, containing twenty entries, but again the names of important individuals and valuable corrodies are totally missing.[52]

So can it be assumed that the corrody system, as it had existed in Outlaw's time, was beginning to die out? Was it that the order had decided to limit the numbers of corrodies granted? Was there no longer a need to do so? Had the Kilmainham house ceased to be such a popular place to stay, and was the order no longer in a position to offer maintenance at a suitably tempting level? In the light of what is known about the rapaciousness of some of the later priors, the second hypothesis seems the more likely. It would appear that the status of the Kilmainham house declined and that the Black Death must be considered a major reason for this decline. The nature of the house – with its concentration of population, its proximity to Dublin, its rivers and mills and accompanying rat population, its openness to infection from travellers returning from other towns – made it a more than suitable breeding ground for the fleas which spread the plague bacillus. The sumptuous furs worn by the wealthy corrodians must, indeed, have been a perfect home for them. (It is somewhat ironic that the more successful Kilmainham was as a centre of hospitality, the more it was at risk from the plague.) If the suggestion of two consecutive priors dying of the plague is accepted, the image of the

Kilmainham house must have been severely damaged. In addition to the plague ravaging the rich and mighty, tenants died and loss of income to the order followed. There is a possible downward spiral in action here. The traditional coterie which existed at Kilmainham was disrupted after Outlaw's death by le Mareschal's replacement by the English outsider, Larcher. Larcher did not have time to establish a network to replace this, dying in 1349. By this stage the Black Death had begun to act as a powerful deterrent to the attractions of a closed, close and crowded community – and the depopulation of the land meant that there was no longer a workforce to keep Kilmainham running at its accustomed level. Internal dissensions within the order had increased and the English priory was attempting to gain control over the Irish house by appointing Englishmen as priors, who were rarely in Ireland long enough to create the network of contacts which Outlaw had used to such good effect. As a smaller number of important people took up corrodies in Kilmainham, fewer and fewer important people wanted to stay there. There is a paucity of sources on the operation of the corrody system in Ireland in the later middle ages, so it is impossible to chart its decline with any certainty. It is unlikely that the system died overnight but by the time of the dissolution of the monasteries in the sixteenth century it was no longer in existence at Kilmainham. In the same way, the history of the Hospitaller order after Outlaw cannot be seen as one of continuous decline – Prior Botiller fought at the Siege of Rouen, with 2,500 men at his command, according to one poem – but the nature of their power changed, and although Prior Rawson, the last of the pre-Reformation priors, was a figure respected by the monarch and council in England, by the time of the dissolution the community at the manor seems to have consisted of no more than a handful of brothers.[53] The lack of evidence and the various external crises which effected the fortunes of the Hospitallers in Ireland make it impossible to make sweeping judgements on the long-term value of Outlaw's 'legacy'. What has been shown is that for a particular place and a particular time Outlaw made use of an existing social construct – the corrody – to support him in what must be seen as a highly successful career. In doing this, he in some sense created and most certainly maintained a very particular type of community in the manor at Kilmainham.

# Conclusion

How far Roger Outlaw was consciously aware of manipulating the community at Kilmainham for his own purposes is a question which cannot be fully answered, given the impersonal nature of the available records. But if Outlaw in a sense used the manor for his own purposes, this must not be seen as necessarily detrimental to the people who lived there. On the contrary, in a very literal sense he brought wealth to the house at Kilmainham and to the people who made up the community – the smiths and brewers, millers and horse-boys as well as the great lords. The institution of the corrody gave security to those servants that were granted one, with the promise of food and shelter in old age and sickness. During Outlaw's time as prior the manor was an economically prosperous and socially active community with a very distinct awareness of and pride in its identity. The house at Kilmainham, home and meeting point of so many powerful men, acted as a centre of political gossip and possibly scheming, and therefore must have played a role in the spread of information – no doubt of various degrees of accuracy – among those who held influence in the colony. On a broader level, Outlaw left the Hospitaller order in Ireland richer than he found it, and in a position of greater power in Ireland. He managed the take-over of the bulk of the Templar lands without antagonising either king or nobles, and managed to remain on good terms with three sets of rulers – Edward II, the Mortimer/Isabella alliance and Edward III. He was tireless in his efforts in the administration of the Lordship, engaging in battle or diplomacy as required, and demonstrated great skill in acting as a go-between between the three very different cultural groups – the Gaeil, the English of Ireland and the English of England – which constituted the Lordship. He was also a major force for containment in a situation of disorder which became much worse after his death. The argument throughout this study has been that his use of the corrody system to tie the interests of the record-keepers of the colony to himself and his order was an important part of his success. It is not, of course, the full reason; Outlaw's own military and diplomatic skills and resources and the external circumstances of the time were also very important factors influencing the course of his career and deserve examination in themselves. However, the fact that the institution of the corrody has not been examined before in this context provides an interesting insight into the way a section of Irish society functioned at the time.

It cannot be said Outlaw lived during a particularly easy or stable period; famine, feuding and outright war were characteristic of his era but he appears

*8.* Effigy of knight in interior of Hospitaller Church at Hospital, Co. Limerick, burial place of Roger Outlaw. (Photograph Jacques Le Goff)

to have had the ability to adapt to these difficult conditions and even turn them to his own advantage. As a born survivor, some of his actions may have been dictated by short-term aims – his use of the corrody system to gain immediate advantage for himself and his order can be seen to have risked burdening Kilmainham with the responsibility of supporting an ageing population in later years – but his career shows how someone who operated from a deep knowledge of the local scene and a network of contacts could keep his position secure. Some of these contacts may not have been ethically pristine, nor, from the sparse and enigmatic information of the records, can it be taken that Outlaw himself was above bending the law or giving or receiving a 'favour.' In this he was no different from his contemporaries.

A final point which must be borne in consideration when examining the career of a man in Outlaw's position is that he himself was very much in control of the information which was recorded and the way it was recorded. He controlled the compilation of most of the *Registrum* and in addition to holding the post as chancellor and keeper of the seal he would have had influence with the secretaries and accountants who kept the government records. The only version of history that is available to us is one which to some degree is controlled by what he wanted to be known. But that too must be considered part of his legacy: his superb administrative ability is mirrored in the extent and excellence of the records of the Kilmainham *Registrum*, which leave the reader with a window into a community as it existed six hundred years ago. Clyn's epitaph, with its emphasis on Outlaw's prudence, graciousness and the benefits he brought to his order is perhaps the most suitable summary with which to end a study of his life:

> On Tuesday, the morrow of St Agatha the Virgin, brother Roger Outlaw, prior of the Hospital in Ireland, died: being then the deputy justiciar and the king's chancellor also, thus discharging three offices at once. He was a prudent and gracious man, who by his own industry and the king of England's special favour and licence acquired for his order many possessions, churches and rents.[1]

# Appendix 1: Corrody and tenancy agreements at Kilmainham

| Folio | Name | Manor | Position | Value of Corrody |
|---|---|---|---|---|
| 69 | Adam De Kyngestone | Kilmainham | Cleric & Notary Public | |
| 103B | Adam De Moure | Kilmainham | Brother | |
| 88B | Alice Le Reve & Mathilda her daughter | Kilmainham | Widow | D |
| 10 | David De Slebeche | Kilmainham | Farrier | D |
| 58 | David the Walshe | Kilmainham | Tenant | |
| 72 | Hamund De Lee | Kilmainham | Keeper of the Park | D |
| 77 | Hamund De Lee | Kilmainham | Keeper of the Park | D |
| 35B | Henry De Stone | Kilmainham | Unstated | B |
| 75B | Henry De Stone | Kilmainham | Pensioner | C |
| 110B | Hugh De Calce | Kilmainham | Cleric | C |
| 25 | Hugh De Nassyntone and Cecilie his wife | Kilmainham | Pensioner | B |
| 113 | Hugh De Saltu | Kilmainham | Pensioner | |
| 96 | Hughe De Saltu | Kilmainham | Canon of St. Patricks | B |
| 110B | Hugh De Saltu | Kilmainham | Cleric | B |
| 85 | John De Grauntsete | Kilmainham | Pensioner | A |
| 112 | John De Grauntsete | Kilmainham | Pensioner | A |
| 90 | John De Horewode | Kilmainham | Pensioner | B |
| 115B | John De Clane (DOM) | Kilmainham | Chaplain | A |
| 74 | John De Hothum | Kilmainham | Pensioner | |
| 111B | John De Hothum | Kilmainham | Pensioner | |
| 26B | John De Hothum | Kilmainham | Pensioner | B |
| 56B | John De Kirketone | Kilmainham | Brother | C |
| 72 | John De Stone | Kilmainham | Servant | D |
| 111 | John Donyng, Roger Lawless, Robert | Kilmainham | Pensioner | |
| 9 | John Le Barbour | Kilmainham | Barber? | D |
| 117B | John Schorthals | Kilmainham | Assessor/Keeper of Fish Pond | D |

| Folio | Name | Manor | Position | Value of Corrody |
|-------|------|-------|----------|------------------|
| 84 | John Son of Ralph | Kilmainham | Chaplain | |
| 44B | Nicholas Dyllesburri | Kilmainham | Keeper | D |
| 88 | Nicholas son of Nicholas | Kilmainham | Butler | D |
| 10B | Peter Le Charpentier | Kilmainham | Carpenter | |
| 11 | Peter Le Charpentier/ De Lodelowe | Kilmainham | Carpenter | D |
| 115B | Richard De Westone | Kilmainham | Brother | |
| 117 | Richard son of Roger | Kilmainham | Janitor | D |
| 22 | Richard Swayne | Kilmainham | Tenant | |
| 71B | Robert De Faringho | Kilmainham | Steward | B |
| 8B | Robert Gutter | Kilmainham | Janitor/ Park-Keeper | D |
| 92 | Robert Son of Thomas The Reve | Kilmainham | Keeper of the Grange | D |
| 97 | Roger De Cryketot | Kilmainham | Chaplain | |
| 93 | Roger Godman | Kilmainham | Tenant | |
| 36 | Roger Jordan | Kilmainham | Servant | D |
| 57 | Roger Jordan & Avicia | Kilmainham | Tenant | |
| 85 | Roger Lawless | Kilmainham | Pensioner | B |
| 31 | Roger Outlaw | Kilmainham | Prior | |
| 59B | Roger son of William De Knohille | Kilmainham | Vendor | |
| 4B | Simon Keepok | Kilmainham | Tenant | |
| 87 | Stephen son of Richard | Kilmainham | Janitor | |
| 45 | Stephen son of Richard | Kilmainham | Janitor | D |
| 97B | Thomas De Camburgh | Kilmainham | Unstated | C |
| 115B | Thomas Louryn | Kilmainham | Chaplain | A |
| 18B | Walter Breghnoke | Kilmainham | Tenant | |
| 9B | Walter De Aloun | Kilmainham | Unstated | C |
| 67 | Walter De Istelep | Kilmainham | Brother/Pensioner | |
| 67 | Walter De Istelep | Kilmainham | Brother/Pensioner | |
| 98 | Walter De Istelep | Kilmainham | Cleric | A |
| 57B | Walter De Kynefare | Kilmainham | Cleric | C |
| 61 | Walter De Kynefare | Kilmainham | Pensioner | A |
| 9 | William BarretteLe Keu | Kilmainham | Servant | D |
| 78B | William Boydyn | Kilmainham | Cleric | A |
| 58 | William Bardelby | Kilmainham | Cleric | |
| 79B | William De Boseworthe | Kilmainham | Cleric | B |
| 93B | William De Boseworthe | Kilmainham | Pensioner | B |

| Folio | Name | Manor | Position | Value of Corrody |
|---|---|---|---|---|
| 113 | William De Chichester | Kilmainham | Pensioner | A |
| 13 | William De Walshe | Kilmainham | Unstated | B |
| 3A | William De Wideworth | Kilmainham | Unstated | C |
| 4 | William De Wideworth | Kilmainham | Tenant | |
| 12 | William De Wideworth | Kilmainham | Tenant | |
| 3A | William De Wideworth | Kilmainham | Unstated | B |
| 114 | William Le Keu of Bernarde's Castell | Kilmainham | Cook | C |
| 29B | William Le Mareschal | Kilmainham | Pensioner | |
| 24 | William Le Mareschal | Kilmainham | Pensioner | |
| 111B | William Le Mareschal | Kilmainham | Pensioner | A |
| 107 | William Le Mareschal | Kilmainham | Pensioner | |
| 59 | William Le Mareschal | Kilmainham | Pensioner | |
| 75 | William Le Mareschal | Kilmainham | Pensioner | |
| 2B | William Le Mareschal (& John) | Kilmainham | Pensioner | |
| 71 | William Le Walleys | Kilmainham | Unstated | |
| 35B | William the Smith | Kilmainham | Smith | |
| 73 | William the Smith of Kilmainham | Kilmainham | Smith | D |
| 106B | William Wlamichio | Kilmainham | Pensioner | A |

# Notes

## ABBREVIATIONS

| | |
|---|---|
| *Administration of Ireland* | H. G. Richardson and G. O. Sayles, *The administration of Ireland 1172–1377* (Dublin, 1963) |
| *Alen's Reg.* | Charles McNeill, (ed.), *Calendar of Archbishop Alen's Register c.* 1172–1534 (Dublin, 1951) |
| *C. Chart. R.* | *Calendar of Charter Rolls* (London, 1903) |
| *Cartulaire General* | Jean Delaville de la Roulx, (ed.), *Cartulaire Général de l'ordre des Hospitaliers de St-Jean de Jérusalem (1100–1310)* 4 vols Paris, 1894–1906) |
| *CCR* | *Calendar of Close Rolls* (London, 1908–38) |
| *CFR* | *Calendar of Fine Rolls* (London 1911–62) |
| *CPR* | *Calendar of Patent Rolls* (London 1891–) |
| *EHR* | *English Historical Review* |
| *Extents* | Newport B. White, (ed.), *Extents of Irish Monastic Possessions, 1540–1541* (Dublin, 1943) |
| *The Hospitallers in England* | L.B. Larking, (ed.), *The Hospitallers in England, being the report of Prior Philip de Thame to the Grand Master Elyas de Villanova for* AD *1338* (London, 1847) |
| *Irish Exchequer Payments* | Philomena Connolly, (ed.), *Irish exchequer payments* (Dublin, 1998) |
| *Narrative* | Thomas Wright, (ed.), *A contemporary narrative of the proceedings against Dame Alice Kyteler* (London, 1843) |
| NLI | National Library of Ireland |
| *Notes . . .* | Charles McNeill, *Extracts and notes from the archives of the Order of St John of Jerusalem 1350–1560.* NLI Ms. 4839 |
| *Papal Letters 1305–42* | W. H. Bliss, (ed.), *Calendar of Papal Registers: Papal Letters vol. 11, 1305–42* (London, 1895) |
| *PRI rep.DK* | *Report of the Deputy Keeper of Public Records in Ireland* |
| *Registrum* | Charles McNeill, (ed.), *Registrum de Kilmainham 1326–39* (Dublin, 1932) |
| RIA | Royal Irish Academy |
| *Riwle* | K.V. Sinclair, (ed.), *The Hospitallers' Riwle* (London, 1984) |
| *Rot. Pat. Hib.* | Edward Tresham, (ed.), *Rotulorum Patentium et Clauorum Cancellariae Hiberniae Calendarium* (Dublin, 1828) |
| *RSAI Jn.* | *Journal of the Royal Society of Antiquaries of Ireland* |

## INTRODUCTION

1 *Cartulaire Général de l'ordre des Hospitaliers de St-Jean de Jérusalem, (1100–1310)*, ed. Jean Delaville de la Roulx, 4 vols., Paris 1894–1906, ii, pp. 536–59.

## THE COMMUNITY AT KILMAINHAM: THE WORLD OF THE MANOR

1 *Registrum de Kilmainham 1326–39*, ed. Charles McNeill, (Dublin 1932).
2 Newport B. White, ed., *Extents of Irish monastic possessions, 1540 –1541*, (Dublin, 1943).

3 RIA, Ms 12 B1 1.
4 *Registrum*, p. 27.
5 *Registrum*, pp 2, 101.
6 *Registrum*, p. 107.
7 *Registrum*, pp 2, 27.
8 *Registrum*, pp 27, 68.
9 For reference to the walls, see *Registrum*, p. 27; for the tower and gatehouse, pp 25–26.
10 See Fig. 2
11 *Calendar of Justiciary Rolls of Ireland- I to VII years of Edward II (1308–14)* ed. Herbert Wood and A. E. Langman; rev. by M.C. Griffith (Dublin 1956) p. 219.

12  *Registrum*, p. 95.
13  *Registrum*, p. 126.
14  See *Extents*, pp 81–82; also the 1212 Confirmation of Hospitaller lands by Pope Innocent in Mc Neill's notes to the *Registrum*, pp 138–40.
15  Fishing was of great significance to the Hospitallers and sometimes a source of conflict with the local population: in 1220 there was dispute over rights to the river Liffey. See J.T. Gilbert and Lady Gilbert, eds., *Calendar of Ancient Records of Dublin*, (19 vols., Dublin 1889–1944), i, pp 160–162.
16  Some smaller buildings at Kilmainham were also of stone: e.g. the stone house given to Hugh de Saltu recorded in the *Registrum* on p. 122.
17  Colum Kenny, *Kilmainhaim* (Dublin, 1995), p. 43.
18  *Registrum*, p. 8.
19  *Registrum*, p. 27.
20  *Registrum*, pp 17, 102.
21  *Registrum*, p. 25.
22  *Registrum*, p. 68.
23  *Registrum*, p. 68.
24  *Registrum*, p. 26.
25  *Registrum*, p. 136.
26  *Registrum*, p. 102.
27  *Registrum*, p. 25.
28  *Registrum*, p. 25.
29  *Registrum*, p. 23.
30  *Registrum*, pp 26–27, p. 68.
31  *Registrum*, p. 25.
32  *Registrum*, p. 107.
33  *Extents*, p. 81.
34  *R.S.A.I. Jn.*, v, (1858–9) p. 444.
35  *Registrum*, p. 126.
36  *Registrum*, pp 8, 84.
37  *Registrum*, p. 70.
38  See Appendix 1.
39  *Registrum*, p. 84.
40  *Registrum*, p. 93.
41  *Registrum*, p. 10.
42  *Registrum*, p. 9.
43  *Registrum*, p. 37.
44  *Registrum*, p. 116.
45  *Registrum*, p. 80.
46  Charles McNeill, 'The Hospitallers at Kilmainham and their guests', in *R.S.A.I. Jn.*, xxiv, (1924) pp 15–30, p. 29.
47  Maria Fitzsimons, The Knights Hospitaller at Kilmainham. (Unpublished B.A. Thesis, NUI Maynooth 1992), pp 15–16.
48  *Riwle*, p. 22, lines 741, p. 23, line 789: *Cartulaire General*, ii. No. 627.
49  *Riwle*, p. xli.
50  Newport B. White, ed., 'The *Reportorium Viride* of John Alen, archbishop of Dublin 1533' in *Analecta Hibernica* no. 10, (1941), p. 184.
51  O'Malawyll, (p. 88) Inyndonull, (p. 36) McColaghty, (p. 49) Ogloeryn, (pp 77, 111) Karrig (pp 60, 67, 90) and Ococran (p. 78) are the Irish names listed in the *Registrum*. It is interesting that all the first names are English.
52  *Registrum*, p. 9.
53  *Registrum*, pp 43, 93.
54  *Registrum*, p. 26.
55  *Registrum*, p. 90.

56  See M. Haren, and Y. de Pontfarcy, (eds.), *The medieval pilgrimage to St Patrick's Purgatory Lough Derg and the European tradition* (Enniskillen, 1988), p. 124, where Prior Frowyck is recorded as entertaining a Hungarian pilgrim at the Kilmainham house.
57  *Registrum*, p. 54.
58  *Cartulaire General*, ii, pp 536–559.
59  See *Registrum*, p. 114 where le Mareschal is described as the prior of the Hospital in Ireland.
60  *Registrum*, pp 30, 56, 72.
61  See for example the conditions of Islep's corrody: *Registrum*, pp 64–65.
62  *Registrum*, p. 123.
63  See M. C. Lyons, 'Weather, famine and plague in Ireland, 900–1500', pp 31–74 in E. M. Crawford, (ed.), *Famine: the Irish experience 900–1900* (Edinburgh, 1989) pp 31–74.
64  *Registrum*, p. 98.
65  K.V. Sinclair, 'Anglo-Norman at Waterford' in Ian Short (ed.), *Medieval French textual studies in memory of T.B.W. Reid* (London, 1984), pp 219–38.
66  The patron saint of the order changed from the original St John the Almsgiver to St John the Baptist.
67  Philippe Aries, (ed.), *A history of private life, vol. ii: Revelations of the medieval world*. (Harvard and London, 1988), pp 16, 56.
68  During the Kyteler trial, William Outlaw wore the livery of Arnold le Poer as a sign of Arnold's support against Bishop Ledrede. See L. S. Davidson, and J. O. Ward, *The sorcery trial of Alice Kyteler*, (New York, 1993), p. 48.
69  Robin Frame, *Ireland and Britain 1170–1450* (London 1998), pp 206–209.
70  A.M. Freeman, (ed.), *Annals of Connacht*, (Dublin, 1944), p. 88.

THE WORLD BEYOND THE MANOR

1  Outlaw is described as a kinsman of the wealthy William Outlaw of Kilkenny in Thomas Wright (ed.), *A contemporary narrative of the proceedings against Dame Alice Kyteler*, (London 1843), p. 3.
2  *Registrum*, pp 4, 14, 20, 33, 45.
3  *Registrum*, pp 61, 82, 103.
4  C. L. Falkiner, 'The Hospital of St John of Jerusalem in Ireland' in *R.I.A. Proc.*, xxvi Sec. C (1907), p. 316.
5  *Calendar of justiciary rolls of Ireland 1308–14* ed. Herbert Wood and Albert Langman, rev. by M. Griffith (Dublin 1956), p. 319.
6  *Calendar of justiciary rolls 1308–14*, p. 47.
7  Philomena Connolly, (ed.), *Irish exchequer payments,* (Dublin 1998), p. 234.
8  *CCR 1313–18*, pp 464–5.
9  *Irish exchequer payments*, p. 246.
10  *CPR 1317–21*, p. 12.
11  *The administration of Ireland*, p. 94.
12  P. Chaplais, (ed.), *The war of St Sardos*, (London 1954), p. 178.
13  *Irish exchequer payments*, p. 293.
14  *Irish exchequer payments*, p. 316.
15  *Irish exchequer payments*, p. 326.

16  *Irish exchequer payments*, p. 329.
17  *CCR 1330–33*, p. 594.
18  *Irish exchequer payments*, p. 365.
19  *Irish exchequer payments*, p. 616.
20  *Irish exchequer payments*, p. 326.
21  *Irish exchequer payments*, pp 378–9.
22  *CPR 1330–34*, p.82. Edward III was crowned aged only fourteen in 1327, but effectively took control of his kingdom after the removal of Mortimer and Isabella in 1330.
23  *CPR 1330–34*, p. 340.
24  *Administration of Ireland*, p. 95.
25  *Administration of Ireland*, p. 95.
26  *CPR 1338–40*, p. 116.
27  *Administration of Ireland*, pp 85–87.
28  *Registrum*, p. 21.
29  *CCR 1327–30* p. 221
30  G. O. Sayles (ed.) *Documents on the affairs of Ireland before the king's council* (Dublin, 1979) p. 131:'*Sire, le priour de Kilmaignan vostre chaunceller . . . del iour qe vostre seal lui fust liverez nous ne avioms eide ne conseil de lui, car il est ocupie es bosoignes del hospital qil ne poet attendre a les voz, et auxint ses possessions sount dispars par tote la terre.*'
31  *Alen's Reg.*, p.167.
32  *Papal letters 1305–42*, pp 131–2.
33  *CPR 1317–21*, p. 12.
34  *CPR 1317–21*, p. 197.
35  *CPR 1327–30*, p. 171.
36  *CPR 1338–40*, p. 90.
37  *CCR 1327–30*, p. 275.
38  *CCR 1327–30*, pp 256, 266.
39  *CFR 1337–47*, p. 85.
40  For a full discussion of the problems of the administration of the time, see the introduction to *Administration of Ireland*.
41  *Registrum*, p. 26.
42  *Registrum*, pp 98, 114, 122, 123.
43  *Registrum*, pp 23, 24, 30, 56, 72, 102, 110, 115, 117.
44  *Registrum*, p. 74.
45  *Registrum*, pp 76, 95.
46  *Registrum*, pp 88, 121, 124.
47  *Registrum*, pp 55, 58, 65, 91.
48  *Registrum*, pp 54, 58, 75.
49  *Registrum*, pp 2, 3, 11, 12, 55.
50  *Registrum*, pp 34, 55, 62, 73, 124.
51  *Registrum*, pp 64, 65, 99, 115.
52  *Registrum*, pp 99–103.
53  J. F. Lydon, *The lordship of Ireland in the middle ages* (Dublin 1972), p. 113.
54  *Papal Letters 1305–42*, p. 241.
55  *Irish exchequer payments*, p. 212.
56  *CFR 1307–19*, p. 74.
57  *Alen's Reg.*, p. 164.
58  *CPR 1313–17*, p. 85.
59  *CCR 1313–1318*, p. 293.
60  *CCR 1318–23*, p. 90.
61  'Catalogue of accounts in the pipe rolls of the Irish exchequer I to X Edward II', *P.R.I. rep. D.K. 39*, appendix, pp 21–74, pp 60–62.
62  *Administration of Ireland*, pp 100–101.
63  *Irish exchequer payments*, p. 270.
64  Mervyn Archdall, *Monasticon Hibernicum – the history of the abbies, priories and other religious houses of Ireland* (Dublin 1786), p.161.
65  *CPR 1321–24*, p. 39.
66  *CFR 1320–26*, p. 46.

67  *CCR 1318–23*, p. 432.
68  *CCR 1323–27*, pp 41, 70.
69  *CCR 1323–27*, p. 287.
70  *CCR 1323–27*, p. 432.
71  *CCR 1323–27*, p. 449.
72  *CPR 1324–27*, p. 197.
73  *CPR 1324–27*, p. 250.
74  *CCR 1327–30*, p. 260.
75  *CCR 1327–30*, p. 266.
76  'Catalogue of accounts in the Great Roll of the Pipe of the Irish exchequer for the reign of Edward III', *P.R.I. rep.D.K. 45*, appendix, pp 24–56, p. 41.
77  *CCR 1327–30*, pp 430–31.
78  *CFR 1337–47*, p. 423.
79  *Papal letters*, p. 326.
80  *Alen's Reg.*, p. 202.
81  *Papal Letters 1305–42*, p. 536.
82  *CCR 1337–39*, p. 362.
83  Sayles, (ed.) *Documents on the affairs of Ireland before the King's Council*, pp 131–2.
84  *Papal Letters 1305–42*, p. 536.
85  *CPR 1327–30*, pp 471–72.
86  *Rot. pat. Hib.*, p. 23.
87  *CPR 1330–34*, p. 4.
88  *Irish exchequer payments*, p. 369.
89  *CFR 1327–37*, p. 246.
90  'Calendar of Christ Church Deeds', 20 *PRI rep. D.K.*, appendix p. 76.
91  *Irish exchequer payments*, pp 353, 356.
92  *Irish exchequer payments*, pp 344, 370.
93  *Irish exchequer payments*, pp 350, 362.
94  *Irish exchequer payments*, p. 370.
95  *CPR 1330–34*, p. 328.
96  *Irish exchequer payments*, p. 334.
97  *Registrum*, p. 27.
98  *Registrum*, p. 3.
99  *Irish exchequer payments*, p. 240.
100  *Irish exchequer payments*, p. 324.
101  *Administration of Ireland*, p. 95.
102  *Papal Letters 1305–42*, p. 516.
103  J. T. Gilbert, (ed.), *Historical and municipal documents of Ireland AD 1172–1320* (London, 1870), p. 93.
104  *CPR 1330–34*, p. 325.
105  *CPR 1338–40*, p. 88.
106  *Registrum*, p. 65.
107  *Registrum*, pp 48–49.
108  Robin Frame, 'Power and Society in the Lordship of Ireland' in *Past and Present* no. 76 (1977), pp 3–33.
109  R.Butler (ed.), *Annals of Ireland by Friar Clyn and Thady Dowling* (Dublin, 1849), p. 29. Clyn is selective rather than formulaic in the adjectives he uses in his obituaries.

OUTLAW AND THE KYTELER WITCHCRAFT CASE

1  Art Cosgrove (ed.): *A new history of Ireland*, vol ii (Oxford 1987), p. 299.
2  James Lydon: *Ireland in the later middle ages*. (Dublin 1973), p. 55.
3  William Carrigan: *The history and antiquities of the diocese of Ossory*  (4 vols, Dublin 1905), i pp

45–57. Carrigan concludes that Ledrede 'well deserves to be ranked among the greatest and most illustrious of the bishops of Ossory'; (p. 56).

4  Norman Cohn: *Europe's inner demons* (London 1975), pp 135–141.

5  Anne Neary, 'Richard Ledrede, English Franciscan and bishop of Ossory 1317–60' in *Butler Society Journal*, ii, no.3 (1984), pp 273–82. Also: Anne Neary, 'The origins and character of the Kilkenny witchcraft case of 1324.' In *R.I.A. Proc.* lxxxiii Sec. C (1983) pp, 333–350.

6  Brennan, James, 'Richard Ledrede, bishop of Ossory – towards a new assessment' in *The Old Kilkenny Review* 1998, pp. 10–19.

7  Thomas Wright (ed.): *A contemporary narrative of the proceedings against Dame Alice Kyteler*, Camden Society, xxiv, (London 1843).

8  Clyn, *Annals*, p.13.

9  Aubrey Gwynn, 'Provincial and diocesan decrees of the diocese of Dublin', *Archivium Hibernicum*, xi (1944), pp 57–71.

10  Anne Neary, 'The Kilkenny witchcraft case', *R.I.A. Proc* lxxxiii Sec. C, (1983), pp 333–350.

11  Printed in Wright's notes to the *Narrative: Narrative*, p. 42.

12  Emmanuel Le Roy Ladurie, *Montaillou* (London, 1978).

13  See Carrigan, *The history and antiquities of the diocese of Ossory* i pp 54–55 where he gives the text of a letter of 1334 from the pope to Edward III, written under the influence of Ledrede and encouraging him to set up an inquisition. See also *Letters from the Northern Registers*, ed. James Raine (London 1873), p. 403 where Edward III complains to Pope Innocent VI that Ledrede had wanted an inquisition set up in England.

14  *Papal letters 1305–42*, p. 461.

15  The Hospitaller charms are discussed in pp 226–227 in K.V. Sinclair, 'Anglo-Norman at Waterford' in Short (ed.) *Medieval French textual studies*, pp 219–238.

16  'Provincial and diocesan decrees', p. 71.

17  *Narrative*, p. 14.

18  Quoted in John Watt, *The church in medieval Ireland*, (2nd. Edition, Dublin 1998), p. 260.

19  *Papal letters 1305–42*, pp 206–7.

20  All the following references to events are taken from the account given in the *Narrative* unless otherwise indicated.

21  *CPR 1318–23*, p. 530.

22  Eric Colledge, *The Latin poems of Richard Ledrede* (Toronto 1974).

23  L. S. Davidson, and J. O. Ward, *The Sorcery Trial of Alice Kyteler*, (New York 1993), p. 29.

24  Robin Briggs: *Witches and neighbours* (London 1996), pp 63–64.

25  *Witches and neighbours*, p. 274.

26  *Cancellarius regis consanguineus dicit Willelmi* (*Narrative*, p. 3).

27  *Propter quod oportuit episcopum cum paucis extranis per loca deserta, montuosa et invia arripere versus Dubliniam* (*Narrative*, pp 16–17).

28  *Narrative*, p. 18.

29  *Narrative*, p. 49.

30  *tantos advocatos juriseritiores* (*Narrative*, p. 40).

31  James Morrin quotes Petronilla as claiming that Roger Outlaw was as worthy as death as she, for he wore the devil's girdle: other sources cite William Outlaw as the subject of this accusation and it is likely to be a mistake on Morrin's part. See James Morrin, 'The Kilkenny Witchcraft Case' *Transactions of the Ossory Archeological Society*, i, (1874–9), p. 235.

32  *Narrative*, p. 37.

33  John Watt, *The Church in medieval Ireland*, p. 24.

34  *Amicus specialis thesauraii*, (*Narrative*, p. 24).

35  Davidson and Ward, *The Sorcery Trial of Alice Kyteler*, p. 66.

36  *Dictus cancellarius prorumpens in lacriamas dixit 'Si in aliquo erratum est, non ex intentione vel malitia sed potius ex ignoranta processit error'.* (*Narrative*, p. 36).

37  G. O. Sayles (ed.), *Documents on the affairs of Ireland before the king's council* (Dublin, 1979), p. 131. It should be acknowledged that the Earl was heavily involved in the feuding with the earl of Desmond at this time.

38  For the full text of Ledrede's accusations against Le Poer see Sayles, *Documents on the affairs of Ireland*, pp 132–134.

39  *Regesta Pontificum Romanorum*, ccxxxi, ed. P. Jaffé, (1885), p. 574.

40  At this time the power struggle between Edward II's favourite, Hugh Despenser, and Roger Mortimer was at its height. In 1327 Mortimer, with the help of Queen Isabella, finally triumphed and deposed the king.

41  See Robin Frame, *English lordship in Ireland 1318–1361*, pp 180–182 and *Parliaments and councils of medieval Ireland* ed., H.G. Richardson and G.O. Sayles, (Dublin 1947), pp 202–203.

42  Evelyn Mullally, 'Hiberno-Norman literature' in John Bradley (ed.), *Settlement and Society in medieval Ireland: studies presented to F.X. Martin* (Kilkenny 1988), pp 328–343, 335–6.

43  J.T. Gilbert (ed.) *Chartularies of St Mary's Abbey*, (2 vols, London, 1894–6) p. 369.

44  Willeby was chancellor of St Patrick's (*CPR 1321–24*, p. 431).

45  *Chartularies of St Mary's Abbey*, ii, p. 369.

46  *Narrative*, p. 17.

47  *Narrative*, p. 18.

48  *Chartularies of St Mary's Abbey*, ii, p. 369.

49  Clyn claims that Petronilla was the first person to be burnt for heresy in Ireland. See *Annals* pp 16–17.

50  *Chartularies of St Mary's Abbey*, ii, p. 361.

51  Sayles, *Documents on the affairs of Ireland*, p. 131.

52  For the full text of Ledrede's accusations against Bicknor see Sayles, *Documents on the affairs of Ireland*, pp 173–7. For his appeal against Bicknor's sentence of excommunication, see *CCR 1339–41*, p. 222.

53  Sayles, *Documents on the affairs of Ireland*, p. 131.

THE 'LEGACY' OF OUTLAW

1  *Chartularies of St Mary's Abbey*, ii, p. 369.

2  *CCR 1333–37*, p. 38.

3   *CCR 1333–37*, p. 679.

4   *CPR 1334–38*, p. 478.

5   *CCR 1337–39*, pp 140, 161.

6   See Robin Frame: *English Lordship in Ireland 1318–1361*, (Oxford, 1982), Chapter 8 for a full discussion of the crisis.

7   *Registrum*, p. 108.

8   Charles McNeill, 'Extracts and Notes' NLI MS 4839, f11, recto, in headed 'Chapters General, 1330, 1332'.

9   *Registrum*, p.124.

10   *Administration of Ireland*, pp 95–96.

11   This and all the following information on posts held in the administration is taken from *Administration of Ireland* unless otherwise stated.

12   A.J. Otway-Ruthven, *A history of medieval Ireland* (London, 1968), p. 269.

13   *Administration of Ireland*, p. 96.

14   *Administration of Ireland*, p. 96.

15   *Administration of Ireland*, p. 90.

16   *CCR 1354–60*, pp 595–6.

17   *Administration of Ireland,* p. 85.

18   *Administration of Ireland*, pp 101–102.

19   *Administration of Ireland*, pp 20–21.

20   *CPR 1338–40*, p. 532.

21   *Registrum*, introduction, p. ix.

22   L.B. Larking, (ed.), *The Hospitallers in England,* (London, 1847), introduction, p. lxxi.

23   *Registrum*, p. 31.

24   Katherine Walsh, *A fourteenth-century scholar and primate: Richard Fitzralph in Oxford, Avignon and Armagh* (Oxford, 1981), pp 267–268.

25   *CCR, 1360–64*, p. 39.

26   NLI, MS 4839, f.xi, headed 'Chapter general at Rhodes, 1330'.

27   Gilbert, *Calendar of the ancient records of Dublin*, i, p. 127.

28   Maria Fitzsimons 'The Knights Hospitallers at Kilmainham,' pp 49–54.

29   *CCR, 1399–1401*, pp 225, 373.

30   See Charles Tipton, 'The Irish Hospitallers during the Great Schism' in *R.I.A. Proc.*, lxix, sec. C, (1970), pp 33–43, p. 38.

31   Ibid.

32   Larking, (ed.), *The Hospitallers in England*.

33   Larking, (ed.), *The Hospitallers in England*, p. lxi.

34   McNeill, Charles, 'The Hospitallers at Kilmainham and their guests' in *R.S.A.I. Jn.*, liv (1924) pp 15–30, p. 18. (Footnote).

35   *Registrum*, passim.

36   See the corrody listed for William de Langford in *CPR 1334–38*, pp 352–53.

37   Larking, (ed.), *The Hospitallers in England*, p. 88.

38   P. Foster, *The Hospitallers at Hampton* (passim).

39   Larking, (ed.), *The Hospitallers in England*, introduction, p. xlix.

40   Larking, (ed.), *The Hospitallers in England*, p. 216. Outlaw also seems to have availed of the services of money-lenders on occasion – he is listed as owing money to Asselinus Simonetti of Luca in 1332 – *CPR 1330–34*, p. 575.

41   *Registrum*, p. 13.

42   Larking, (ed.), *The Hospitallers in England* p. xli. It is possible that some of the money payments listed in the *Registrum* may also have been for this same purpose.

43   NLI, MS 4839 f.12, headed Chapter General at Rhodes 1335.

44   Even in the early fourteenth century there were popular complaints against the fine robes and shoes and splendid horses of the Hospitallers; see 'The order of fair ease' in Thomas Wright, (ed.), *The political songs of England from the reign of King John to that of Edward II*, (London 1889), p. 140.

45   A.J. Otway-Ruthven, *A history of medieval Ireland* (London 1968), p. 268.

46   *Registrum,* introduction, p. xv (my italics).

47   *Registrum*, pp 32–33.

48   *Registrum*, pp 87–104.

49   *Registrum*, pp 105–114.

50   *Registrum*, pp 114–124.

51   *Registrum*, pp 124–129.

52   *Registrum*, pp 129–137.

53   *Extents*, p. 82.

CONCLUSION

1   Clyn, *Annals*, p. 29.